Pathways to a Radiant Self

A Journey of Growth and Discovery
with the Chakras

Kathy Pike
www.PathwaystoRadiance.com
www.coachpike.com

Pathways to a Radiant Self
A Journey of Growth and Discovery with the Chakras

Important: Please note that this book is not intended to substitute for the advice of physicians of other health care providers. It offers information to help the reader work with health care and personal development professionals to achieve greater wellness and understanding of the body mind connection.

PTR Publishing
www.PathwaystoRadiance.com

Copyright © 2002 by Kathy Pike

Cover and Content design by Anita Jones, Another Jones Graphics
Cover Image by Glen Halack
Editing by Lis Tanz Harrison

ISBN 0-9721638-0-8

Library of Congress Control Number 2002109208

Printed in the USA

table of contents

acknowledgements

I thank the many individuals who have supported me,
encouraged me and coached me in the process of writing this book.
Anita Jones, thank you for being a bright light that transformed the
material into a wonderful visual presentation. Lis Tanz Harrison,
thank you, for your dedication and many hours of editing.

I express gratitude and appreciation for the many people
who have been my mentors and teachers;
you have helped me to heal and see myself.

Most of all I thank the many people who have shared
their lives with me on their path of discovery and growth.
Thank you for your trust.
Without you this would not have been possible.

foreword

*T*he chakra system has intrigued me for over 10 years. It was first introduced to me in 1992 at the Heartwood Institute in Northern California where I began my path as a massage therapist. In 1995 I studied polarity therapy with Anna and John Chitty in Boulder, Colorado; at this time my knowledge of energy fields, elements, and chakras expanded. The chakra model has never been far from my consciousness since it entered my world. I found that in my healing sessions there were patterns where people held pain in their body from the emotional issues that challenged them. I used the chakra system to better understand these patterns and how I might help facilitate increased wellness for my clients.

In 1997 I began my training as a Personal Coach. As I began to support people in developing a life they wanted, I also noticed patterns of beliefs and thoughts that limited their ability to create the life they dream of. These naturally aligned with the chakra system. I started to examine other personal development models and found that many of them focused on different aspects of the chakra system.

The chakra system is a model I am continuously applying to all aspects of my life, my relationships, the organizations I observe and work with, politics, the dynamics of the world, and the universe as an energetic form. For me, this model provides a never-ending process of learning and understanding of patterns, insights, commonalities, and applications to life. The purpose of this workbook is to introduce the model to you. It is my hope that this workbook helps you to explore the energetic system that lies within you and how your external life reflects the vitality of that system.

This system is ancient and complex. This workbook is my humble interpretation of the system from my unique viewpoint and my own spiritual path. I have blended my love for nature, energy, personal growth, and esoteric knowledge into a workbook for you to explore and play with, as you like. This workbook is not intended to replace any other materials available to you on this topic as much as it is a support for you as you study and read other sources. The intention of this workbook is to spark an interest in how you can grow and flourish from exploring the chakra system, the elements, and the choices you can make that shape you and your world. The primary focus is to generate energy and awareness of where you may be lacking vitality. Generating energy is only the beginning. Once your chakras are activated you will want to find the fine line of balance and expression that allows your being and life to flow magically from you.

It is my hope that this workbook will provide you the depth and breadth of knowledge and concepts to support you on your life path.

how to use the
pathways to a radiant self workbook

This book is designed to help you tap into your vital life energy. It includes an outline and explanation for the seven chakras (energy centers) that are located in your body. Simply by bringing your attention to these areas, you will begin to shift your energy and your life. Continual work and action steps will increase your chances of experiencing profound and lasting results. The results you will see may include a greater sense of health and well being, better mental clarity, increased prosperity, and the ability to attract a mate or establishing your right livelihood. The focus of this book is to blend aspects of the body, mind and spirit together to help you achieve the vital energy you need to create whatever you are wanting in your life.

Contents of Workbook:

Mind Body Inventory Sheet

The Mind Body Inventory Sheet will help you to begin the process of connecting your mind and body. Often, there are patterns and connections between how we think and act and how this energy manifests in our body. The Mind Body Inventory sheet is designed to help you begin to make these connections. As you move through each chakra chapter, review your notes on the Mind Body Inventory Sheet. Explore possible connections and patterns in your life and how you might want to shift them. As you deepen your understanding of the chakra system, your understanding of the mind body connection will also deepen.

Chakra Chapter Cover Pages

Each chakra chapter has a cover page with an illustration of the chakra covered in that chapter. This is your space to tap into your creative nature and give the chakra its appropriate color. I suggest you use several different shades of the same color for each chakra. These variations will produce depth, variety and texture in your drawing. Let yourself have fun during this process. Explore how you feel, physically and emotionally, when you have completed each chakra graphic. I personally found that when I work with the chakra symbols in an artistic manner, my personal energy level increases tremendously. Allow your creative self to come out. Don't be shy in exploring different creative things. You may even want to build a collage into this page. Glue photos, magazine photos, color swatches and pieces of fabric on to the page to bring the energy and color of the chakra to life.

Chakra Assessments

Each chakra chapter has an assessment to help you explore your energy level in that particular chakra area. Answer each question to the degree that it is true for you at this time. Tally up your scores at the end. Use the scores below as a guide to the health of that chakra and how you might want to take action to increase the vitality of that chakra.

80-100   Your vital energy in this chakra center is excellent at this time. Review the chapter to maintain your healthy balance.

60-79   Your vital energy in this chakra center is good at this time. Take some actions to increase your possibilities and energy levels.

40-59   Are you experiencing difficulties in certain areas of your life? Focus on this chakra to begin to balance and re-energize yourself.

20-39   Your vital energy is zapped in this chakra. Take some action today!

0-19   Yikes! Get into action now. You may want to seek professional counsel.

After each assessment you will find a worksheet with questions to help you further explore the vitality of the chakra.

Chakra Text

Each chapter contains a section of written text to help you understand the essence and purpose of the energy represented in the chakra.

Chakra Themes

Each chapter includes a few pages with the main themes for the chakra. These themes include information such as the chakra element, color, location, core shifts, challenges, balanced characteristics, goals, as well as the signs of emotional and physical imbalances/balances. As you read through these materials, circle or mark anything that concerns you. This will help you to see where you can focus your developmental energy for each chakra.

Activities to Explore:

Each chakra chapter includes a list of activities to explore as you begin the process of re-energizing that chakra center. These exercises will help you to connect with and understand the element and quality of energy that is stored in the chakra center.

Follow your instincts and go at your own pace. Begin with what sounds like fun and then proceed to what looks most difficult or undesirable. You may discover that what you are resisting exploring is ultimately keeping you at the same energy level. Be brave and explore as many activities as you can within your personal safety. When you choose to take a risk and experience unknown territory, create the appropriate support for yourself.

The main focus is to get your energetic system expressing its true potential. Consider this program a 'life energy training' program. The activity lists are the training steps. These steps will strengthen you and help you create and maintain the vital energy for each chakra center and your life in general.

Shifts for the chakras and journal questions

Use these two areas as you have the other sections. Explore and discover which pieces resonate with you or catch your attention. Begin working with these pieces. These two areas will help you to further peel away the things that are stealing energy in your system. Keep peeling the layers until you are alive and well, creating exactly what you want everyday.

Chakra Summary Worksheet

When you reach the Chakra Summary Worksheet you will have reviewed and explored many aspects of the chakra. This worksheet is provided at the end of each chapter to help you summarize your learning, so that you may make tangible commitments to the changes that will support you in your vital life energy. Use this worksheet to track your commitments and your progress. When you work with others, share what you have set your intentions on and hold each other accountable for your development. You are the one that must take the first steps in shifting the energy of your life. Once you have made a few steps you may notice that things get a little easier and go more smoothly. If so, great! You are on your way!

On the other hand, you may also experience the opposite. For instance, you may feel like everything just got harder and the challenges seem too big. Know that this is also part of the process. Not all things in life come easily. Sometimes the things that we put forth the most energy for are the most rewarding to achieve and therefore worth the efforts. Congratulate yourself for the courage to step forward and begin the process of making changes. It is good to remember that you are the only one that can take the very first step. And, ultimately your success is up to you!

Good luck and welcome to the discovery of your life's energy!

the human energetic body

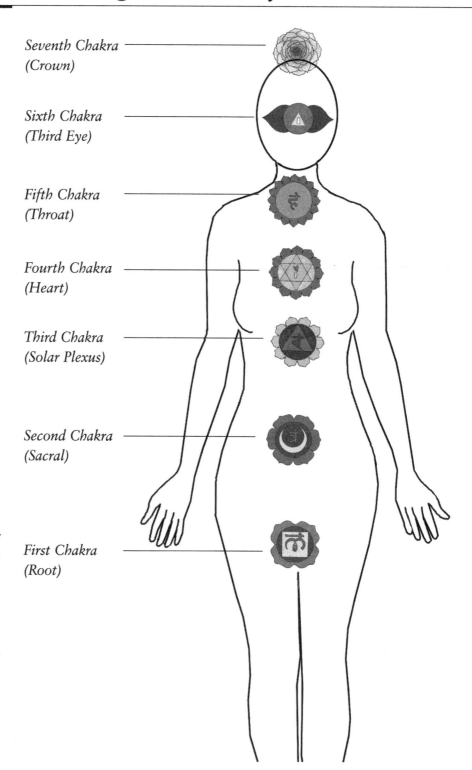

Seventh Chakra
(Crown)

Sixth Chakra
(Third Eye)

Fifth Chakra
(Throat)

Fourth Chakra
(Heart)

Third Chakra
(Solar Plexus)

Second Chakra
(Sacral)

First Chakra
(Root)

"Major centers of both electromagnetic activity and vital energy are recognized in indigenous cultures the world over. In the Huna tradition of Hawaii, they are called Auw centers; and in the Cabala, they are the 'Tree of Life' Centers. In the Taoist Chinese Tradition the term is Dantein, and in yogic theory they are called 'Chakras'."

William Collinge,
Subtle Energy

statement of intention

*B*efore continuing on please take a moment to contemplate why you have decided to work with this book. There may be something you wish to gain in the next few weeks. You may be seeking clarity on something, you may wish to create something new in your life, or you may want to feel more life balance and personal energy. In the space below, write a statement of intention for taking this journey of discovery.

Examples of Statements of Intention:

- My intention for using this workbook is to better understand my energetic being and how to get more energy in my life.

- My intention for using this workbook is to energize myself and take my business to the next level.

- My intention for using this workbook is to release behaviors that may be holding me back and to embrace new perspectives.

Your Statement of Intention:

Balance / Energy / Health

"There is only one corner of the universe you can be certain of improving, and that's your own self."

Aldous Huxley

an introduction into the chakra system

The origin of the chakra system.

Originating in India 4000 years ago, the chakra system is rich with influences from the Hindu religion and culture. The symbols, words, theories and scriptures that are the roots of this system are saturated with the mystical nature of its heritage. One need not study the Hindu religion to understand the system. The system can be studied and applied in many different ways. Western cultures are embracing the chakra system more and more as yoga is growing in popularity. The meaning of the word yoga is "to yoke." The focus of yoga is to engage the physical body and breath to expand levels of consciousness, thus bringing the body and spirit together. In this way the chakra system becomes the missing bridge between spirit and matter. The purpose of this workbook is to introduce the themes of the chakra system, to help you apply the concepts and theories into your life and to deepen your understanding of how you are uniquely designed.

The purpose of the chakra system.

The ancient chakra system is a model that represents the integration of body, mind and spirit. The chakra system provides a map to follow on the path to personal growth. You may be focused on rising above the limitations of your life to better understand spiritual realms, or you may be on a path to bring spiritual concepts into your everyday life. Regardless of which pathway you are on, this model helps you to explore many layers and levels of the human experience. These pathways lead you to the exploration of the physical human body, the emotional body, the sensing body and the intellect. The chakra system blends all of these in a manner that provides you with a system to understand and deepen your sense of self. By using this system as a model for personal growth and development, you explore yourself from the inside out. You merge your sense of self on many levels and you live a life based on what is authentic and unique to your own nature.

"The chakra stimulates and integrates conceptual realization of spiritual insights. It is the bridge between feelings and thinking, between the concrete and the abstract."

*John Selby,
Kundalini Awakening*

What is a chakra?

Chakra is a Sanskrit word meaning wheel or disk. A chakra, as a wheel or disk, moves or rotates, creating a spinning vortex that produces and expresses energy. All spinning matter creates a force. Imagine an eddy in a river, a tornado, or water draining from the sink. You can see and sense the energy that is moving within the vortex in each of these situations. This visual is similar to how a chakra center might appear within the body. It has a circular shape, is in motion, rotating and moving, expressing and creating bio-energetic activity that is derived from the nervous system and spinal column.

You can see chakra shapes all around you. Roses, starfish, the cross section of tree trunks, and mandalas of many religions and traditions all reflect a circular pattern and design. The Lotus flower is the traditional symbolic flower for the chakra system. The petals on each chakra symbol represent the opening of the flower. The first chakra has only four petals while the seventh chakra has 64 petals. Each chakra center also has its own color, element and rate of vibration or energy quality.

There are seven major chakras within the human body. These centers are lined up vertically from the base of the spine to the top or crown of the head. Each chakra functions individually and also is intrinsically connected with the rest of the system. A chakra exists where several planes, points, and lines of light meet. If you look at a map of the United States you see many lines identifying roads that lead from one city to the next. Where there are cities, the lines converge and the area appears denser. Cities are where many people travel to and from, and where a larger population lives. Chakras appear within the human body in the same way. The chakra is where there are several intersections of energy concentrated in one area. These areas, or energy centers, become the centers of activity where exchanges of information and processes occur, much like the activity and exchange of goods and services that occur within a city.

If you look at a drawing of the nervous system in the human body you will see that the nerves of the human body are attached to the spinal column. As these nerve pathways move away from the spinal column, they become finer and finer as they reach out into the body. In some areas there are many fine nerve pathways that form into little bush-like formations called ganglia. Nerves transmit the activity of the body carrying the messages back to the main nervous system. When these messages enter the main nervous system signals are given to the body so it can prepare and respond to changes in the internal and external environments it is experiencing. The fine nerve ganglion combined with the activity of the endocrine system is the creating area of a chakra. As you look at the drawing of the human body's nervous system you will see that these bunches of fine nerves correspond to the same areas where the seven main chakras reside.

"Miracles do not happen in contradiction to nature, but only in contradiction to that which is known to us in nature."
St. Augustine

"Energy is always there, whether we think we are aware of it or not."

John Chitty,
Energy Exercises

Can I touch my chakras?

Chakras are not something we can touch on the physical plane. You can sense the energy within the chakras and many people receive intuitive information about the colors and vibrancy of each chakra. A chakra is a center where interpretations of life experiences are processed. It is through these centers that you take in the energy of your life experience and where you put energy back out into the world. The movement of energy gives way to sensations within the body. These sensations give clues to the health of the chakra centers. You can experience sensations that correlate with the chakras; you may feel tightness in your throat when you have not expressed yourself; you may feel butterflies in your stomach before you attempt a new activity; or, you may feel like your heart is broken or tight when you feel hurt by other people's words or actions. These are the chakra centers speaking through you, giving you information about how you process, experience, and formulate the world around you.

The function of a chakra.

The seven chakras of the body are oriented vertically from the base of the spine to the top of the head. Each of these centers has its own theme or topic for processing and releasing information and energy. Experiences are sensed and processed within these centers, a person's interpretations of their experiences are rendered, and beliefs are established. When a child seeks to become an individual he may assert himself. If the child is continually punished or scolded for being assertive, he may begin to associate being assertive with being scolded or wrong. The child then learns to disown his natural ability to be assertive. As an adult he may be challenged with the ability to show up as a powerful, decisive and assertive person. Aspects of one or more chakras may be out of balance and lacking the energy needed to create what he wants.

"The amount of spirit a person has is determined by how alive and vibrant he is, literally by how much energy he has. The connection between energy and spirit is immediate."

Alexander Lowen, M.D.,
Bioenergetics

The chakra center that processed the original experience and information has an established way of responding to similar life activities or experiences. Sometimes the manner in which the center processed the information is useful; other times the manner of processing is not useful. Either way, as an individual grows from childhood into adulthood, the chakras interpret events of life and establish a program for future interpretations. As you explore each of the chakra centers, you are working on shifting the patterns of how you assess and respond to the world (energy) around you. As you shift your behaviors and beliefs, the energy within each chakra center becomes more balanced. You then create the energy to live a more healthy, vibrant and rewarding life.

How to understand the energy as it applies to life.

As you observe and connect with the quality of energy in each chakra center, you begin to see how you process information and lead yourself through life. You will see how you go about making decisions, taking actions and experiencing relationships. There is a contracted state and an excessive state of energy in each center. When the state of one's being is contracted, the energy is pulled inward, often holding back or not engaging with others or avoiding a situation. When the energy in that center is excessive, the individual may move forward in an unbalanced way, overpowering others, talking over others, being overly emotional or working excessively. When you explore the energy of the polarities, the contracted state and the excessive state, you learn how to bring those energy expressions into balance. A balanced state is full of vitality and health in the body and mind.

The themes for each chakra.

These seven centers are uniquely different; each has its own theme and expression.

The first chakra, the earth or root chakra, is located at the base of the spine and relates to being connected to the earth. As such, it has the densest energy of all chakras. It is within the first chakra that one learns how to be grounded and present to the activities, experiences of life, and to one's needs and desires on a physical survival level. The first chakra is about having a deep-rooted sense of the physical being. It is here that you learn how to care for yourself, be safe at all times and stand on your own two feet. The first chakra is the foundation from which you grow your life. Without a solid connection to this center you may be constantly moving toward a goal, only to find yourself never quite realizing that goal. Or, conversely, you may struggle to get on your path and take any movement in any direction. It is here that the beliefs acquired early in life are challenged in adulthood.

The second or sacral chakra is located in the lowest part of the belly near the female reproductive areas and just slightly above the first chakra. This is the center for our sexuality and sensuality. The energy for this chakra is water. Water flows and moves, carves and reveals. One's secret desires, passions and creativity lie within this center. The pathway to reach these desires is to understand one's feelings and emotions and to use this understanding as a tool in the exploration of life experience. If emotions and feelings are not experienced, energy is repressed and it is difficult to live fully and authentically. Instead, the energy of life is focused on keeping feelings and emotions

"We are either initially attracted to or repulsed by people, places and things. We eventually want to move either toward whatever makes us feel curious and safe, or away from what threatens us."

*Johanna Putoi-
Senses Wide Open*

11

repressed. It is in this energy center that the seed of your life creation is held. Without connection to the emotional body, it is difficult to identify passions and desires. The passions and desires of what you want to create in life are what move you forward.

The third chakra, the solar plexus chakra, is just above the second chakra and located near the upper area of the stomach at the solar plexus. This is the center for one's vital energy, personal power and will. It is in this center that the transformational processes of life are engaged. You cannot create anything in life without getting yourself into action. The third chakra engages your ability to act so that you can transform your ideas into reality. The ideal is to take actions based on your integrity; this aligns you with your authentic nature and creates momentum for a higher sense of self-respect, self-reliance and self-worth. By establishing what is a right action, through proper mental functioning and activity, one establishes the energy of personal power.

Next is the fourth chakra, the heart chakra. The heart chakra is centered in the body at the heart area. This is the center for self-acceptance, unconditional love and connection with others. The energy represented here is the energy of connection. It is the heart energy that is the glue of the world. Through love we connect with others and ourselves on the deepest levels. When you reach a place where you are fully engaged with loving energy, your mind shifts from "how do I fit into the world," to "how may I serve others and help?" Heart centered individuals are in relationship to all that is around them, they are people of a caring nature, concerned for others, mankind and the environment.

At the base of the throat is the fifth chakra, the throat chakra. The theme of this chakra is communication and creativity. The energy here is experienced through your communications, how you speak, when you speak, how you listen and what you hear. What you speak becomes your reality. It is here that you ultimately become the creator of your life. If I ask you to walk to the park with me, I create the opportunity for time together. If I ask you to leave me alone for the afternoon, I create solitude. Words, language and the tone of our speech are a powerful request to the universe of what we seek to create. Becoming aware of how you communicate, the words you use, and how well you hear others, helps you to refine the quality and direction of your life path.

The third eye is the name for the sixth chakra, which is located right between the eyes on the forehead. Your eyes help you to see and recognize shapes, colors and textures of the world. You also see patterns and recognize things according to what your eyes are accustomed to perceiving. When you can see the patterns in life, the things that happen over and over, you can begin to shift the cause or root of what attracts these recurring themes into your life, thus creating something different. You learn how to shift your perspective to change your world. This center also helps us to better understand hidden messages in the form of our dreams, synchronicities and symbols. This center is the center for intuition and insight.

The last chakra, the crown chakra, is located on the top the head. Here one connects to the energy of the universe, expanding and connecting with a deeper understanding of one's consciousness. By understanding your thoughts and your beliefs you understand how you are connected to or disconnected from your spiritual nature and the universal energy. It is in this chakra center that the energy and power of silence is explored.

"Stop trying to figure out why someone acts the way he or she does. The powerful question is: 'Why do I react the way I do?'"

Susan Jeffers

It is my observation that there is wisdom and knowledge for each of us to gain within each of these centers. As you drop into the body and use the body as a source of wisdom, you hear new messages that have a profound effect on your choices and your life path. To fine tune your sense of your energy body and how your energy body moves and responds to life, you gain a sense of self that is deep and sustaining. You connect to your own spirit as it is expressed through energy. The chakra system provides a model of understanding during this process of exploration. The themes of each of the chakra centers give you a place to explore and understand on many levels. As you explore these concepts and processes you learn how to shift the energy of your expression, thus shifting how you create the life that you want, from the inside out.

How energy flows through the system.

Each chakra has its own quality and flow of energy. There are also other flows of energy that relate to and affect the system. There are two vertical currents of energy in the body; one moves upward from the earth into the first chakra, flowing upward toward the crown chakra, and exiting out into the universe. The current upward represents the pathway of liberation. It is by moving upward, through each chakra, that you liberate yourself from the mundane aspects of your existence. This upward flow allows you to connect with your spiritual nature and the universal energy. The second current, moving downward, is the pathway to manifestation. The energy runs downward, coming from the universe entering into the crown chakra, passing through each individual chakra to the first chakra, out the first chakra and back into the earth. This is the pathway where you utilize your intuition and spiritual aspects to manifest what you choose to create on the physical level. While the movement, up or down, of each pathway is distinct, they work in concert to create your life.

The power of working with the chakra system lies in your willingness to explore your life from several different perspectives. These perspectives include exploring your physical body, your emotional intelligence and your understanding of spirituality and energy concepts. This model weaves in all aspects of your life and lets you explore and unwind your life's path in a fashion that is rewarding and transformational. It is a system for continual evolution. As you observe yourself, you become more aware of how you participate in the world. You also explore how you create your life through your intention. Where you place your intention, you create movement. Through understanding and exploration of your energetic being and the themes of the chakra system, you begin to understand how your external life takes its form.

This workbook focuses on the themes of each chakra center, how these themes are expressed in life, and what will help you to connect with each center, bringing it into full vitality. It also explores the quality of the energy and element expressed in each chakra, giving you the opportunity to see how it is expressed in your life and in your body. For each center, you will choose an exercise, tool or process to help you explore the understanding of the center. Select those that are most natural for you and what you are most drawn to explore.

"Many of us are working with people who truly want to find deeper meaning, connection, right livelihood and purpose. All of these relate to finding what is inside us, what is our essential nature and true expression. To do this we must not only coach our clients about increasing their awareness of the exterior world but also of their interior world. A world that they may have disconnected with."

Ann Weiser Cornell, Ph.D.
The Power of Focusing

key questions for each chakra

Consciousness/Beliefs (7)
What is your spiritual orientation?

How do you quiet your mind? What is your spirituality?
How do your beliefs create your life?

Intuition/Patterns (6)
How do you use your intuition and wisdom?

How do you play and engage with your inner voice/intuition? Can you
see your potential, the possibilities? What patterns re-occur in your life?

Communication/Creativity (5)
How do you create your life through communications and intentions?

What is true for you? What is your communication style? How do
you create your life through your words? How do you relate to your
body intelligence?

Relationships/Love (4)
What is your relationship to love?

How do you love yourself and receive love from others?
What makes you feel connected to others?
How do you maintain and nurture long lasting loving relationships? How
do you serve humanity and spirit? What do you most want for others?

Power/Will (3)
What makes you feel vital, strong and powerful?

What does the word 'integrity' mean for you?
Do your actions align with your thoughts and words? What makes you feel
vital and strong? What is your relationship with your ego?
How do you speak to yourself?

Unconscious Creativity/Desire (2)
What are your deepest desires?

How do you honor and express your desires? Where is your life not flowing? What is your secret dream? How much of your life is based on your decisions? How do you express emotions?
What do you feel passionate about in life?

Survival/Attitude (1)
Do you have a structure that will support the growth of right livelihood?

What supports and nourishes you? What is your attitude about what you do and do not have? How do you take care of yourself emotionally and physically? What makes you feel safe and secure? How do you stay present and in the moment?

mind body inventory sheet

1. Write down a challenge you often experience in your life. Give full detail of what happens, when and where it happens, and how you feel when this event occurs.

    Weight, I can't give up chocolate. I feel deprived when I can't eat it. I get anxious, If I don't have any I'll look for something w/ choc. in it or I'll go buy something

2. What would you like to receive clarity on? What would you like to know or have resolved? *Why I was born built like a man*

3. Now take a moment and scan your internal body. What are you most aware of? Where do you sense the most amount of energy? Where might you feel tight? How are you holding yourself?

    I feel... Im most aware of my aches/pains. Sense most energy abdomen. Feel tight - knee Holding self tensely

4. Now, while remaining present to the sensations in your body, write down the question that you would most like to have the answer to.

    Why I wasn't born beautiful

5. Looking at the list below, circle five to seven key phrases that best represent areas you struggle with or areas where you need skills improvement.

One
Attitude of gratitude
Accepting what is
Trusting how things will happen
Feeling secure and safe
Attitude of abundance
Self reliance

Having a sense of belonging
Prosperity
Connection with body
Maintaining good physical
    health
Being fully present and in the
    moment

Two
Ability to feel emotions
Expressing emotions
Expressing desires
Moving from desires and vision
    into action

Letting go of guilt
Tapping into creativity
Keeping emotions contained
Feeling vital, happy and alive
Being able to flow with life

Three
High level of integrity
Consistent, directive action
Personal, balanced authority
Vitality and energy

Self-esteem, self respect,
    self-confidence
Doing what you say you will do
Asserting yourself
Being less aggressive

Four
Releasing judgment
Self-love
Compassion with self and others
Relationships
Joy

Loving unconditionally
Bitterness, jealousy
Releasing self-judgment
How to serve others
Feeling isolated

Five
Speaking your truth
Creative expression
Listening
Saying exactly what you mean
Being heard

Finding your voice
Articulating your vision
Living your vision
Creating what you want
Speaking up for yourself

Six
Intuition
Trusting your gut feelings
Understanding dreams

Identifying the patterns in your life
Identifying your intuitive language
Paying attention to symbols

Seven
Letting go of expectations
Releasing the attachment to
    outcomes
Understanding of universal
    connections

Shifting your belief system
Spiritual connection
Quieting the mind
Letting go of having to 'know'

6. Using the list below, circle the physical ailments that you have experienced in your body. Then, go back through the list and check the ailments that have been in your family history. Keep in mind these may be ailments you have already circled.

<u>One</u>
- Sciatica
- Lower back pain
- Eating disorders
- Problems with lower digestive ✓
  system

- Problems with teeth and bones ✓
- Weak legs ✓
- Chronically tight legs

<u>Two</u>
- Loss of appetite
- Kidney infections ✓
- Sexual dysfunctions

- Knee problems ✓
- Lower back pain

<u>Three</u>
- Chronic fatigue
- Kidney infections
- Allergies
- Hypertension ✓
- Problems with the gall bladder ✓

- Digestion problems ✓
- Heart disease ✓
- Diabetes
- Skin disorders
- Eating disorders

"Often the body speaks that which the mind refuses to utter."

Mabel Todd

<u>Four</u>
- Cancer ✓
- Asthma
- Pains in the chest
- Pain between the shoulder
  blades ✓
- High blood pressure ✓
- Shallow breathing

- Sunken chest
- Chest colds
- Heart problems ✓
- Lung problems
- Weak immune system

<u>Five</u>
- Sore throats
- Thyroid problems ✓
- Jaw problems ✓

- Neck aches
- Hearing problems ✓
- Sinus infections

<u>Six</u>
- Glaucoma
- Headaches ✓
- Poor vision ✓

- Poor memory ✓
- Nightmares

<u>Seven</u>
- Epilepsy
- Brain tumors

7. Review the last two questions. What numbered sections have the most 1, 3, 4, 6
circled and checked words in them? Return to question number three, write Back Colon Bladder
the area of your body that your attention went to as you engaged the energy
of your challenge. As you begin working through the chakra chapters, pay
close attention to the chapters that reference these body areas.

CHAKRA	BODY AREA	LIFE DEVELOPMENT	GOALS	OVERLY ACTIVE	BALANCED	UNDERACTIVE
Crown Chakra (7th) Sahasrara *Thought*	The crown of the head: Upper skull, cerebral cortex	Selflessness	Expanded consciousness	Overly intelligent, spiritual addiction, confusion, dissociation	Wisdom, knowledge, consciousness, spiritual connection	Learning difficulties, spiritual skepticism, limited beliefs, materialism, apathy
Third Eye Chakra (6th) Ajna *Sight*	What we see with: Eyes	Intuitive intelligence	Ability to see what can not be seen with eyes	Headaches, nightmares, hallucinations, delusions	Ability to clearly see 'what is', patterns, use of intuition	Poor memory, poor vision, can't see patterns, denial, overly rational
Throat Chakra (5th) Visshuddha *Vibration/ether*	The parts of the body involved with communication: throat, ears, nose, jaw, mouth, neck	Personal expression, the power of choice, expression of truth	Expression of self-knowledge, passion and creativity	Arrogant, shameless, tyrant, excessive talking, inability to listen, stuttering	Clear, graceful communication, creative expression, expression of will	Fear of speaking, poor rhythm, worthless, less than, shamed
Heart Chakra (4th) Anahata *Air*	Areas that provide transportation and connection to the rest of the body: heart, chest, lungs, circulation	Compassion, acceptance and forgiveness of oneself and others	Healthy, nurturing relationships with self and others, a sense of balance and connection	Codependency, poor boundaries, possessive, jealous, impatient, super mature, dissatisfied	Compassion, self-acceptance, self-love, loving actions, feelings and thoughts toward self and others	Shy, lonely, isolated, lack of empathy, bitter, critical, depressed, jealous, super immature
Solar Plexus Chakra (3rd) Manipura *Fire*	The areas of the body that digest and process what we consume: diaphragm, digestive system, muscular system	Self-esteem, self-confidence, and self-respect	Live with purpose, effectiveness, endurance and self-respect	Blaming, resentful, explosive, controlling others, judging, dominating, aggressive, scattered, constantly active	Vitality, spontaneity, strength of will, purpose, high level of self-esteem	Weak will, poor self-esteem, passive, apathetic, sluggish, fearful, blaming self, controlled by others
Sacral Chakra (2nd) Svadhisthana *Water*	That which flows in the body: sexual organs, bladder, circulatory system	Uncovering what motivates oneself, expression of feelings and desires	Experiencing pleasurable and creative activities, flowing through life	Overly emotional, poor boundaries, obsessive attachments, compulsive, isolated	Pleasure, healthy sexuality, ability to express desires, emotions and feelings	Rigidity, emotional numbness, fear of pleasure, needy, dependent, possessive
Root Chakra (1st) Muladhara *Earth*	Bones, skeletal structure, pelvic floor	Creating environments to support the growth of right livelihood	Create physical health, fitness, grounding, stability, and attitude of abundance	Monotony, hoarding, greed, materialism, invulnerable, paranoid, defensive	Stability, grounding, physical health, prosperity, trust	Fearful, lack of good boundaries, resistance, vulnerable, self-doubting, defensive, lack of discipline, trust

First Chakra

Muladhara

the first chakra assessment

Assess the vitality of this aspect of your life energy system. Place an "X" under the number that best represents the current status of each statement for you. Five is the highest ranking of level of truth. One represents the lowest level.

	1	2	3	4	5
I am in good health and I am very seldom sick.				X	
I have a solid life foundation to launch my dreams and visions.				X	
I trust in the unfolding process of my life.		X			
I am highly aware of all aspects of my physical body and take actions that care for and nurture its growth.			X		
When I do feel sick, I take the necessary time to take care of my physical body.				X	
My living and working environments are peaceful, creative and nurturing for me.		X			
I am a very grounded person. I am fully aware and present in the moment.					X
People understand and respect my personal space.				X	
Organization is not an issue for me. I focus easily on the tasks at hand.			X		
My energy is consistent and well directed.			X		
I feel that I have plenty of everything I want and need, including money, time, love, food, friends, and physical exercise.					X
I belong to a group or community of like-minded individuals that support me on my path.				X	
I view the world as a place full of abundance, for me and for others.			X		
I trust that the world will provide for me all that I need and want.		X			
I have established and am living a rewarding and satisfying career and life.			X		
I am seldom fearful or anxious about how things might turn out in the future.		X			
In general, I feel very safe and secure on a daily basis.			X		
I am disciplined in various areas of my life.				X	
I love my body. I feel comfortable with the size and shape of my body.		X			
It is easy for me to accept suggestions and criticism from others.	X				

Total of all Columns   1 2 6 7 1

1 · 10 · 18 28 5

Guide for Results:

80 – 100:	Your vital energy in this chakra center is excellent at this time. Review the chapter to maintain your healthy balance.
60 – 79:	Your vital energy in this chakra center is good at this time. Take some actions to increase your possibilities and energy levels.
40 – 59:	Are you experiencing difficulties in certain areas of your life? Focus on this chakra to begin to balance and re-energize yourself.
20 – 39:	Your vital energy is zapped in this chakra. Take some action today!
0 – 19:	Yikes! Get into action now. You may want to seek professional counsel.

the first chakra assessment questions

1. Which statements caught you off-guard, made you slightly uncomfortable, raised an eyebrow or caught your attention? *weight*

2. How do you feel after doing this assessment? *anxious*

3. What areas of the assessment do you feel confident about?

   I'm grounded

4. What aspects of the assessment raised an emotional reaction in you? If so, what was your response? *criticism*

5. What areas do you see that you might want to put some attention on releasing, healing, fixing, or creating? Please list these with three steps to support your growth in each area.

   accept. critic

the first chakra: muladhara

Of the seven chakras, the first chakra has the slowest vibration and densest energy. It is called Muladhara and is located at the base of the spine in the pelvic floor. This chakra's color is red and the element is earth. The earth is the most solid and dense element we experience. The purpose of the first chakra is to provide a structure and foundation from which we can grow and expand into the life we want to create.

The earth is the primary structure for all that exists on the planet. It provides a solid foundation for things to grow and expand. In your life, you need a base of energy that is solid and supportive so that you may go out into the world and create what you want. The first chakra provides the opportunity to embrace the energy that will support you in this process. When your first chakra center is healthy, it reflects a person who is well grounded and who has an attitude of abundance and possibility. When it is not healthy, you might appear to be unfocused, have difficulties achieving goals, have 'pie in the sky' thoughts, be disconnected from your body, and often experience excess thoughts of fear or lack.

"People without this foundation of Earth may not be able to deal with the practical everyday life and may become caught up in dreams or indulge in emotional excesses."

Franklyn Sills,
The Polarity Process

The energy of the earth moves very slowly. It is an enormous dense mass. When you touch the earth in a garden, you find moist, rich, dark soil. It feels lovely in your hands. You sense how well the seeds planted in this soil might grow. Normally, crops flourish in Middle America. Yet, during the dust bowl years of the 1930's many crops were lost. When the earth's conditions are drier, the soil becomes thin and dusty and often lacks the qualities needed to grow healthy crops. Take a moment to imagine how these two opposite earthy qualities would feel in your hands.

Drier soils can become fertile growing areas. They need the vital ingredients to bring the soil to a place of richness that will allow growth. It might take several seasons of adding other fertile materials before the harvest begins to pay off. Observing the quality of your life's soil, the things that support and nurture your growth, will help you to determine how easy or difficult it might be for you to create the life you want.

When plants grow, their roots reach into the earth for support. Once this support is felt, the seed then shoots its fresh green growth to the sky coming into its own form of expression. As the plant matures, it creates more green growth and blossoms. More roots grow to support the additional foliage. There is a balance between what is beneath the earth and what is above the earth.

Your life is no different. You need a healthy place to plant your roots so you can then venture out into the world and create what you want. The energy of your life moves from the earth into your first chakra, upward through your whole being, to the seventh chakra and out into the world. Life energy also moves back into your being, through the seventh chakra, down through the first chakra and into the earth. You might imagine these streams of life energy reaching from your body into the earth, establishing your "energy root system." One stream of energy provides a sense of grounding and the other stream sends you nourishment. The current of energy must flow in both directions for optimal results. By creating a strong bond to the earth energy you become grounded in the present in your physical body. You must first cultivate a sense of being grounded and connected within your own being to grow the roots of energy that will support you on your path and life development. To be present means to still the mind and to sense life from within the body through the sense of smell, taste, hearing and the sense of feeling vibration or energy. To be fully present is to be open to the energy that is within the body, and to be willing to engage, converse and integrate the physical sensations as part of one's life experience. Being in your physical body is the primary pathway to a stronger sense of self and a stronger sense of feeling well rooted.

"The body and being inside you were originally designed to work seamlessly together. One "body-self" moving naturally through the world."

Johanna Putnoi, Senses Wide Open

The family provides the original foundation and structure for life experiences. As one grows to become an adult, the ideologies and beliefs that were developed in early life are released. The adult then chooses and establishes the philosophies, values and beliefs that service and support the growth of the adult life. The practices of early life often are replaced with new habits and practices of the adult life. This first chakra energy center is the base of your life and the foundation from which all else grows. Tending your life soil, taking care of what nourishes you and feeds you, will ensure a life of self reliance.

Along with these qualities you also need to develop an attitude that provides the opportunity for your personal growth and expansion. You will need to look closely at the lens you hold in front of you and the way in which you view the world as a whole. Do you see the world as a friendly place where you may play and create from your heart, or do you see a world filled with limitations and restrictions, keeping you small and unworthy? There is a lot to build in the first chakra energy area and when done right, the new supportive foundation carries you to a healthy and abundant life.

The energy of the first chakra is represented in the densest matter within the body. The bones, joints and teeth all provide the structure and foundation for the body to live and move around in. This energy center is about being in the physical body and having a physical experience on earth. We experience life through the physical body by our instinct, our physical needs, and sensations. Our body takes up physical space. Are you aware of the space you are in? Being connected to the body allows you to be fully engaged with the process of life itself. To nurture and love your body is to have a relationship, in the deepest way, to your physical space and your right to be here on this earth. By increasing one's awareness of the body and physical health through proper self-care, one takes responsibility for their health. As actions are taken to provide for the body, a person learns that they are self-reliant. Self-reliance increases awareness and confidence. Ultimately these actions are the catalyst for the integration of the body and spirit. To leave the body behind, to neglect it, is to be denying your own self on a continual basis. It is to be denying life itself.

"In order to increase your energy and partici-pation in life as fully as possible, you must culti-vate an awareness of your body."

Michael Reed Gach, Greater Energy at Your Fingertips

When you are well connected to and caring of your body, you take time to mend when you are sick or injured. You notice the subtle signs that indicate you are run down and tired and that you may have a cold. Noticing these signs is the first step, as are caring deeply for your health and providing yourself the time and care you need to heal and strengthen the core of your life. It is about loving and nurturing your self. A loving attitude brings loving energy into the cells of your body, your body will respond to your attitude. Once you love and nurture yourself you have the ample energy to love and nurture others.

Your body will let you know when you do not love it. Your body knows when you ignore it. Your body will keep telling you what it needs until it gets what it needs. Yet many people will ignore these simple messages and requests of the body, ignoring the container that they reside in. If you ignore these messages, you may first become accident prone, stressed, or tired. This may turn into sickness, chronic illness, or negative weight changes (over or underweight). After months and years of ignoring these pleas and messages, your body may bring you to severe disease and illness. Any of these are signs that your first chakra energy is out of balance. To get back into balance, you must focus on listening to the messages of the body and respond appropriately. If you do not, you will find you will have to focus on recovery, continuing to lose your life energy because you are focused on the pain and inconvenience of your ill health. Notice the attitude you carry now about the organic container you live within.

Daily self-care habits and appreciation for your physical body are imperative to the health of your first chakra. There are two positive results of daily self-care actions. The first is that when you become disciplined in your self-care, you can transfer these acts of discipline to other areas of your life. Discipline is a learned skill that supports you in whatever you want to create. Learning to be disciplined is learning to be present and willing to do what needs to be done to accomplish something. The second result of being disciplined is that the daily self-care actions compounded over time produce good health and become a way of life. Discipline requires you to do the same task over and over to achieve a result that is sustaining and rewarding. Imagine what your life would be like if you always experienced good health and happiness with your body everyday. Imagine the excess energy this would create that you could funnel into another area of your life. Poor self-care zaps you of your full potential. Discipline is the investment of your time to create the energy potential of a brilliant future. Begin the process today to build a body that can carry you through life with ease.

Other areas of your life may also provide grounding and structure. Your living and working environments are where you spend the majority of your time. When you feel happy, safe and secure in these environments you are full of energy for other aspects of your life. Creating an environment that supports you and reflects your inner being is important. Often a thorough cleaning of your home and office can provide an enormous shift in your personal energy. Clean out the garage, closets, drawers, and spare rooms. Discard all items that you do not use. Repair or replace what you do use. If there is anything in your environment that drains you, get rid of it. These items might include projects you have not finished (and likely never will), broken appliances, items that have missing pieces and piles of magazines and papers that you someday want to go through (and more than likely will never get to). These piles of undone things, broken objects and unnecessary items drain your energy on very subtle levels. When you live with these things day in and day out, you become numb to the energy drain. You often can also fall deeper into the drain by beating yourself up every time you walk by these objects. These things remind you of what you have not done instead of what you might be able to do, if you weren't so focused on what you have not done! Don't let your environment steal away your vital life energy and focus. Diligently remove from your life what does not serve you. These small actions support you in creating a better life. Each day be conscious of the energy of your space and the things you have in it.

"Great things are not done by impulse, but by a series of small things brought together."

Vincent Van Gogh

It is one thing to have the things you need to live life. It is another thing to show gratitude for all that you do have. Often it is easy to compare with others. You can easily wish for a bigger house, more money, more time, more food, a nicer car, or better clothing. When you compare and wish for that which you do not have, you are sending a direct message to the universe. The universe hears, "I don't have enough." The universe then provides you with exactly what you are focused on and you essentially get more of 'not enough.' You move into a negative flow of energy because you are focused on what you lack. This act demonstrates to the universe that you lack the trust that you will be provided for at all times. You need to open your eyes to how you are being provided for! The first step is to focus on what you *do* have and show appreciation for it. This is called gratitude. This shift in your attitude brings you to a place of trust. You enter into a positive energy flow. When you see how the universe is providing for you, then you become a co-creator with the universe, you acknowledge the unfolding of your own life in its divine order. You essentially are embracing the goodness in life, that you are thankful, and that you trust the process. The universe responds to this attitude by providing you with more of what you are focused on. Since you now focus on the good things in your life, many more good things will begin to show up. You are now on the pathway of inner abundance and trust which will lead you to outer wealth and happiness.

By developing an attitude of gratitude for what you have, you let the universe know you are focused on the positive aspects of your life. Whatever you focus on, you get more of. Learn to appreciate what you have and be fully present with what *is* in your life, regardless of what you might see others doing or having. This can be a very humbling experience and it is also the gateway to creating abundance. Name five things you are grateful for every day of your life from this day forth!

There are two ways to be in life. One is to be in love and the other is to be in fear. When you live in fear, you become anxious of what may happen to you in the future or what might recur from the past. You worry. When you live this way you are not embracing the earth energy of the first chakra. Earth energy is in the here and the now. It is about being grounded and present. Fear and anxiety create a feeling of not being grounded. By living in fear and anxiety, you lose your life's stability. This is guaranteed to create situations in your life that will support your fears and anxieties. Mastering your fears and how they run you will ultimately set you free. Fear can control you and stop your forward movement or growth. As long as fear runs you, exterior circumstances might change, but the end result or feeling will stay the same. The result is that you are a gerbil in a cage that you designed.

"Fear is not the present, but only the past and future."

The Course of Miracles

Some individuals may experience getting stuck. They may actually feel they cannot make movement toward creating the life they want. They may stay in the repetitive patterns reinforcing the same results day after day. As an adult, one makes choices about how to view life and how to create their reality. Removing the layers of fears leads us to the thought patterns from which the fear emerged. Often, fears are based on beliefs that emerge from the family of origin or past experiences. To heal the wounds of the past is to release the old patterns of energy in your system. Reprogramming your mind with the beliefs that will provide you will possibility and opportunity, establishes a primary aspect of your foundational life structure. Identify your greatest fears, deal with them head on and learn how to rebuild a structure that is supportive to the path you wish to experience from this point on.

The base chakra represents your connection to your body and your environment. This energy is expressed in your ability to trust, be present and work through limiting beliefs and fears. It is here that we also explore the sense of belonging. When you were young, you knew where your home was and where you belonged. As an adult you may want to establish a new sense of connection and belonging. You must redefine for yourself where your home is and what group of people you want to belong to. This requires that you know what is most important to you in your life. The community that you choose to join will share these same values and desires. You then get to hang out with people who understand you and want to support you. Wow! What energy boosts you will experience! Developing a strong sense of community or belonging to a community will strengthen your foundational energy of life and give you a stronger sense of yourself and your abilities. Without this community, you will lack the support and love from others that will help to propel you forward in the most difficult of times.

The first chakra is your base energy chakra. This chakra grounds you, provides structure for your life and challenges you to look at your core beliefs. Look around in your life and see what is working for you and what is not. What supports you and what does not? How does your environment reflect your personality and sense of self? How do you care for your body? Do you have an attitude that invites abundance and right livelihood into your life? Be kind to yourself and nourish yourself in this process. Become fully present to the message of your body and the messages of your life. Remember, this structure and base energy is what will hold you up in the world. It may take a lot of time to get the pieces working smoothly, but once you do you will grow tall and bright like a redwood.

"Everything can be taken from a man but one thing: the last of the human freedoms — to choose one's attitude in any given set of circumstances; to choose one's own way."

Victor Frankl,
Man's Search for
Meaning

first chakra details

Element:	Earth
Sanskrit:	Muladhara, *mula* means root and *adhara* means support
Color:	Red
Location:	Base of spine
Corresponding areas:	Coccygeal plexus, dense matter in body such as bones and teeth, spine
Theme:	Survival/Attitude
Core Shift:	I have and create what I want in the world
Challenge:	Feel fear and take risks

Balanced Characteristics:

A stable, well-grounded individual who demonstrates the ability to manifest right livelihood and prosperity through a sense of stability and right attitude.

Signs of Imbalance:

Too much/Expanded	*Too little/Contracted*
Avoids involvement	Disconnection from body
Paranoid	High level of vulnerability
Hoards, greedy	Self-doubting
Materialistic	Cannot take action
Sluggish	Anxious and worried
Unmoving	Attitude of lack
Lack of community	Lack of discipline with self
Extremely slow to take action	Lack of good boundaries
Dependent on money for security	Difficulty focusing/spacey
Defensive	
Resistant	

Physical Symptoms:

Underweight, obesity	Osteo-arthritis
Disorders of the intestinal system	Eating disorders
Disorders with the bones and teeth	Problems with the knees, feet, legs, spine, or buttocks
Sciatica	

Signs of Balance:

- Is fully present in the body and uses the body as a source of wisdom and personal power
- Achieves goals and manifests life vision or purpose
- Has a sense of trust and security with money and life in general
- Able to exchange information and ideas with others easily

- ❧ Willing to engage with and help others and does so with ease
- ❧ Takes excellent care of health and body with a good diet and exercise
- ❧ Feels supported by others (community) on life path
- ❧ Has resolved and is free of past family issues
- ❧ Can easily focus on the tasks needed to build life dream
- ❧ Accepting of limitations
- ❧ Willing to let go of material items as source of inner worth, happiness and security
- ❧ Models excellent self-care

Goals:

- ❧ Achieve a sense of security and safety through grounding and attitude
- ❧ Achieve a solid loving relationship with the body

Activities to explore:

- ❧ Heal all past emotional wounds and addictions through 12-step programs or counseling
- ❧ Create a solid, grounded foundation and environment (living and working)
- ❧ Develop consistent and stable daily self-care practices
- ❧ Embrace an attitude of gratitude for what you have (regardless of quality or quantity)
- ❧ Develop a sense of trust that (God, Spirit, the Universe) is supporting you through your life
- ❧ Develop strong boundaries
- ❧ Journal daily
- ❧ Practice consciously grounding the body (Use the Daily Root Meditation, page 34)
- ❧ Participate in activities that create a sense of being grounded: walking, yoga, hiking, gardening, rock hunting, archeology digs, backpacking, etc
- ❧ Receive physical healing touch such as massage, chiropractic care, Rolfing
- ❧ Clean up your environment by organizing possessions and fixing or replacing broken items and throwing out items that no longer serve a purpose
- ❧ Join and belong to a community of people who share the same interests

shifts for the first chakra

From...	To...
"I must do this work, I do not have a choice."	"I live a life based on right livelihood."
"I am ungrounded, lack self-care and am often fearful."	"I am fully grounded and nourished."
"I am often frustrated with not having enough."	"I accept, embrace and have gratitude for what I have."
"I seldom feel supported."	"I am fully supported in my life."
"I lack the reserves (time, money, structure, nourishment) to build or create anything in my life."	"I have plenty of reserves to create what I want."
"I must comply and compromise so that I belong."	"I connect with and have a strong bond with a group of people of my choice."
"When is this going to happen?"	"Everything happens perfectly."
"But this is not how I wanted it."	"Things turn out perfectly, I embrace what is."
"Things are much like they were in my childhood."	"I have grown myself into a mature person with the life I want."
"Sometimes my life feels frantic, there is never enough time."	"I am grounded and present to life. My sense of time feels expanded and pleasant."
"If I didn't have all my material goods and financial savings, I would fear life."	"I have material goods for extra joy and comfort. My sense of security is based on my inner strength and sense of self."
"I can't have _____"	"I can have and create what I want."
"My body? What do you mean, am I in my body? Isn't everyone in their body? Let me think about that."	"I love my body, care for it well, and remain present to the messages and sensations it sends me."

Questions for journal work:

- What nourishes you?
- When do you feel safe?
- What frustrates you in your life?
- Where do you feel limitations or constraints (money, relationships)?
- What are the signs that your body needs attention?
- What in your home makes you feel warm and comfortable?
- What makes you feel secure?
- How does your home reflect your essence?
- What things do you do to care for yourself and your body?
- Who in your community supports and honors you?

- What physical sensations do you enjoy in life?
- What holds you back from creating abundance in your life?
- If you had everything you wanted in life what would be different?
- Who would you need to be to have what you want to have in life?
- What do you feel like when you are truly present and in the moment? What do you notice?
- How would you feel if you lost your home, your finances or your job?
- When do you feel grounded? What are you doing when you have this feeling?
- What things do you do in a disciplined manner?
- What in your life might need to shift to create what you want in the world?
- What helps you to stay focused? When do you lose your focus?
- Where do you belong? What group of people do you connect with?
- What past family experiences do you have yet to resolve?

Keywords:

Home	Family	Discipline
Attitude of abundance	Stillness	Grounded
Survival	Body	Tribe
Trust	Belonging	Gratitude

engaging with the earth energy

To be connected to the earth energy is to be grounded. Many times you may find that you are not as grounded as you would like to be. Maybe there is too much to do, not enough time, lots of distractions, or a fear about being fully engaged and inside of your own body. Below you will find a grounding meditation to help you feel the earth energy and the power of being grounded. Practice this meditation daily for one week and notice any differences it makes in your life. How do you feel afterward?   How does it change how you communicate with others and how you make your decisions?

Daily Root Meditation

While you are standing, place your feet shoulder width apart. Plant your feet firmly into the floor with your weight evenly distributed through your whole foot from your toes to your heel. Take a deep breath in; bring oxygen deeply into your lungs as your stomach extends outward. Fully exhale, allowing your stomach to go back to its original position. And again, take a deep breath in, and then exhale all of the air out of your lungs. And one more time, slowly breathe in and then slowly exhale. Now, take a moment to stretch your spine. Imagine that there is a string attached to the top of your head that is being pulled up. As this happens, your spine slowly stretches as it follows your head and your neck. While keeping your spine stretched in this way, slowly drop your shoulders, pulling them toward the ground and away from your head, your neck and your ears. Continue lifting your spine and dropping your shoulders — lifting and gently stretching — lifting and lowering your shoulders.

Now, slowly drop your right ear to your right shoulder and gently rotate your head forward and around to the other side, stretching your left ear to your left shoulder. Then, ever so slowly, rotate your head back, stretching the front of your neck, and gently lift the tip of your chin to the ceiling. And one more time, rotate your right ear to your right shoulder, slowly and gently rotate your head forward and around to the other side, stretching your left ear to your left shoulder. Then, slowly rotate your head back, stretching the front of your neck and gently lift the tip of your chin to the ceiling. Now bring your head into its natural comfortable position. Please let your eyes gaze down as you lower yourself into your chair.

Once in your chair, take a deep breath, closing your eyes and bringing your awareness into your body. Now bring your awareness to your legs and feet. Re-adjust your sitting position so that you feel very comfortable and your spine continues to feel comfortably lifted and stretched toward the ceiling.

Place your hands on the top of your knees or on the sides of the chair. Your feet are placed firmly on the floor, knees bent at a 90-degree angle. Slowly lift your heel and roll the weight to the top of your toes and then lower the weight back to the floor. And, once again, lift your heel, bringing the weight to the front of your foot onto your toes, gently pushing your ankles forward and away from you. Slowly lower your feet. Firmly make contact with your foot onto the floor, feeling every part of your foot connect with the floor, your toes, the ball of your foot, the outside edge and the heel. Become very aware of the full contact of your foot on the floor.

Now, push the soles of your feet into the floor as much as you can while remaining seated. Release. Once again, bring your awareness to the soles of your feet, pushing firmly down into the floor. You may feel the backs of your calves tighten, your thighs tighten and your buttocks may be tightening. And release. Once again, push your feet firmly into the floor. And release. And one last time, push the soles of your feet into the floor. And release.

Bring your awareness into your body and follow any sensations you may be having. Bring your awareness to your breath, making sure you are breathing deeply and evenly. Feel the sensations throughout your upper body and your lower body, in your hips, your legs, and your knees, calves and feet.

Now, imagine that there are cords are attached to the bottom of your feet. These cords are a part of you and allow energy to move gracefully from you and also to you. Imagine these cords reaching down through the floor, through the foundation of the building, and into the layers of the earth. Going deeper and deeper through the layers of the earth and into the very center of the earth. Imagine these cords firmly connected to that center. Imagine your energy, an essential part of your being, traveling along these cords. Imagine your energy going deeper and deeper into the earth feeling the rich, moist, solid texture of all the layers of earth. It is deep, slow, secure, and safe.

Imagine the energy moving back up through these cords, through each of the earthy layers, through the foundation of the building, the floor, and back in through your feet coming up into your legs. Breathe deeply as this slow-moving, consistent mass of energy moves from your legs, to your hips, into your stomach, through your solar plexus and into your heart. And breathe in as this wonderful energy fills your arms, your hands, and your fingers. Continue to breathe deeply as this energy moves through your whole body.

Imagine this energy filling you up, supporting you and nurturing you. Feel the connection to the earth as it feeds you the vital energy you need and want to sustain a vibrant life. Breathe in deeply, imagining the cords from your feet keeping you fully connected to the earth, feeling safe and fully present. Breathing deeply, continue to sustain these wonderful, connective, warm feelings. Pause here for a few minutes and enjoy the connection.

Staying fully connected with the deepest part of the earth, continue to breathe slowly in and out. When you are ready, slowly open your eyes. Maintain the lovely connection you have created as you begin to come back into the room. Remember this feeling and return to it in your day-to-day life when you become disconnected, ungrounded or when you have a quiet moment.

my first chakra summary

1. The insights I have about my first chakra are...

2. What I would like to focus on with regard to the first chakra is...

3. The three things I am willing to do to bring this chakra into balance and vitality are...

    1.

    2.

    3.

4. The behaviors and patterns I am willing to process, explore, release or give up are...

5. I am grateful fo...

Second Chakra

Svadhisthana

the second chakra assessment

Assess the vitality of this aspect of your life energy system. Place an "X" under the number that best represents the current status of each statement for you. Five is the highest ranking of level of truth. One represents the lowest level.

	1	2	3	4	5
I am an expressive person, fully in touch with all of my emotions.			X		
I move about in the world with flexibility and grace.		X			
Change does not scare me nor disappoint me. I see change as an opportunity for growth.			X		
My livelihood has evolved from my desires, creative expression and sense of purpose.			X		
I do not feel guilty about choices I make. I live a guilt-free life.		X			
I easily balance the pleasures and the responsibilities of my life.			X		
My appetite for sex, food and life in general is very good.			X		
I have a well-balanced sex life.		X			
My life is based on what I want and desire and not the desires or opinions of others.			X		
People seldom tell me that I am overly emotional and/or sensitive.		X			
My emotions are clear to me and I can sort them and express them easily.			X		
I understand that people come and go in my life and I do not fear when they go.		X			
I define myself by who I am, not by whom I am with.			X		
I lead a life that feels exciting, joyful and creative.			X		
I know what my personal needs are and how to get them met.			X		
I have experienced my creative thoughts manifesting into tangible creative projects in my life.		X			
I engage with an activity that I feel enthusiastic about several times per week.		X			
I do not use my sexual energy inappropriately.				X	
I am empathetic of others and their emotional states.				X	
I have good emotional boundaries.				X	

Total of all Columns | 58 |

Guide for Results:

80 – 100:   Your vital energy in this chakra center is excellent at this time. Review the chapter to maintain your healthy balance.

60 – 79:   Your vital energy in this chakra center is good at this time. Take some actions to increase your possibilities and energy levels.

40 – 59:   Are you experiencing difficulties in certain areas of your life? Focus on this chakra to begin to balance and re-energize yourself.

20 – 39:   Your vital energy is zapped in this chakra. Take some action today!

0 – 19:   Yikes! Get into action now. You may want to seek professional counsel.

the second chakra assessment questions

1. Which statements caught you off-guard, made you slightly uncomfortable, raised an eyebrow or caught your attention?

   surprise at guilt I hold

2. How do you feel after doing this assessment?

   too lowa score

3. What areas of the assessment do you feel confident about?

    *my empathy*

4. What aspects of the assessment raised an emotional reaction in you? If so, what was your response?

5. What areas do you see that you might want to put some attention on releasing, healing, fixing, or creating? Please list these with three steps to support your growth in each area.

   healing

the second chakra: svadhisthana

The second chakra is called Svadhisthana and is located in the reproductive areas of the human body. Orange is the symbolic color of the second chakra and the element is water. Your body is composed of approximately 80% water. The chakra center, with water as its element, profoundly affects how you live in the world. This chakra provides you the space to explore your ability to feel and understand your emotions, your ability to flow in life, and your ability to connect with your deepest level of creative desires.

Water is one of the most vital resources on the planet. It provides the vehicle for the transport of all vital nutrients to and within plants and living organisms. Without water a plant is limp and cannot hold its structure. With too much water, a plant looks washed out and loses its luster. A balanced amount of water provides the opportunity for vital growth and full expression of the plant. A balanced second chakra in the human body will reflect a person who is in touch with his/her feelings and a person who has the ability to flow in all aspects of his/her life.

Water flows and moves, carves new territory and brings life to seeds that are dormant. Flowing water remains healthy, while stagnant water becomes dark and full of bacteria. The same principle is true for the human body. When the fluids of your body are moving, the body is constantly cleansed as liquids are pumped through the lymphatic system, thereby generating the growth of healthy cells. When the fluids become stagnant the whole system slows and disease is more likely to present itself. Water is a major part of your physical system, the balance of the water element is vital in the process of creating excellent physical and emotional health. When the energy of the second chakra is out of balance, you might experience high levels of emotional turmoil, poor boundaries, lack of any emotions at all and the lack of desire and passion.

"If there is no movement there is no life."

Franklyn Sills,
The Polarity Process

Emotions are the fluids of our non-physical life. When you are sad you might cry but, conversely, when you are happy you might also cry. These two emotional extremes are expressed through the physical body. The tears, the fluids of your body, release and flow as the emotions are expressed and the energy is shifted. Being in touch with and expressing your emotions is a key aspect of the natural flow of your being. Emotion is *energy* in *motion*.

Emotions give movement to life; they are the undercurrent and motivating force of your life expression and purpose. The first chakra helped you to get present and grounded. You increased your self-care and created a safe and secure environment to exist in. The second chakra energy focuses on moving the individual into the world by feeling, sensing and engaging with the things that bring great pleasure and satisfaction. The foundation of the first chakra supports the movement expressed in the second chakra. It is through understanding how you feel and your willingness to explore and express your feelings that you can reach into your soul and find the seed to your life purpose.

Unrecognized emotions and feelings can cause tidal waves and hurricanes in your inner being as they swell and you resist them. This pattern creates a situation in which you may isolate yourself repeatedly from your feelings or people who ignite these feelings, until the force behind the emotions becomes unmanageable, like an inner tsunami. Leaving the tsunami untamed allows its power to grow and grow. The resulting dynamic is an inner struggle and frustration that requires an enormous amount of energy to control, and keep at bay, on a continual basis. This energy turns back into the body and the soul creating a deadening of the spirit that may result in sickness or disease.

Professional help is sometimes needed to process and understand emotions and feelings. Unresolved past traumas can be packed with emotional charges. These emotions are waiting to be released. The resistance to releasing the emotions can often feel bigger than the emotion itself. If you resist, you stop the flow of your life energy. Learning to understand what you are feeling, processing how you want to feel and responding to situations are the key skills to develop.

As a child, you may have been discouraged from or not allowed to express your emotions. You may have hid them to protect others or yourself. Then, as an adult, you may experience difficulty reconnecting to your emotions or you may have feelings of guilt about the emotion you are experiencing. Feelings of guilt can arise when a person experiences negative emotions such as anger and frustration. Feelings of guilt can also arise when one wants to feel lighter and more joyful emotions. Often people are most blocked in creating what they want because they do not feel they have the right to feel so good! Guilt is the plug to the flow of the second chakra. You have the right to your feelings and your desires. You have the right to have them. You also have the responsibility to learn how to manage and express them in productive ways. When you feel guilty about your feelings, you block your emotions and passion, thus resulting in an inability to create and to know what it is you want to create. In order to live a rich life, you must embrace your emotions and learn how to express all emotions in a healthy balanced way. In a sense, you must develop your own emotional intelligence. This can be highly challenging for the individual who was raised in a repressive environment.

The process of exploring your emotions may not require professional therapy. Often, people find body-oriented therapies a wonderful way to get in touch with their emotions on a physical level. Emotions live in the cells of the body. In order to experience your emotions you must be comfortable with "being" in your body. Living in your body may entail retraining the way you focus your attention. Bringing your attention inward to the sensations that are present in your body provides a gateway to your emotional being. Exploring your body sensations increases your wisdom and sense of inner self. Bringing your attention inward to what your body is expressing reconnects you with your natural flow; it gives attention to what your body wants you to experience. Body sensations could be expressed with words such as tingle, twitch, thickening, expansiveness, heat, contraction, pulsing, sharp, throbbing, and numbing. These sensations are the gateway to understanding the emotional being and connecting to the body wisdom. To slow down the rate of perception and feeling is to increase one's awareness and level of consciousness. In doing so, a person becomes highly aware of their feelings and responses from the inside out. This level of awareness provides a strong foundation for all life experiences. If we do not know what we are really feeling, then we certainly can not be "real." Using the Body Mind process at the end of this chapter will help you to start distinguishing the levels of expression in your feeling and emotional being.

"The first step is to have the person identify what they feel, to place their attention on what is occurring in their bodily life. Attending to what we feel takes us out of our heads and into the energetic currents of our body."

Richard Strozzi Heckler, Anatomy of Change

Water can be extremely cleansing. You can see this on ocean beaches or in city streets after a downpour. Water is a powerful force shaping both your physical and emotional worlds. The human lymphatic system processes toxins in the body by removing them through a system of moving water and fluids. The cells of your body carry many different particles and toxins such as foods you have eaten, creams you have put on your skin, elements you have breathed into your lungs, and the thoughts and feelings you have. Feelings are powerful forces that mold and shape your life. Any unspoken words or feelings must be recognized and released for your system to function in a place of freedom and power. If you hold onto these feelings, you stop the flow of your natural energy and the water element in your body slows.

When you hold onto unexpressed feelings you grasp the essence, or vibration, of that feeling. Every thought we have has a measurable quality of vibration. The cells of your body integrate the essence and vibration of your thoughts and feelings. For instance, when you do not allow yourself to feel the anger you have about a person or a situation, those angry thoughts and feelings remain in your body. The energy of the thoughts and feelings permeates your cells and the vibration stays with you. The bottom line is that they are contained in your being. You own them while refusing to recognize or communicate with them. Thus you become the angry person. The more you refuse to feel the anger (or any other negative emotion), the more you keep that vibration in your body and the more you become what you are rejecting. The result is you become the angry person you see others to be.

Resolving past issues with family and friends is a must for the vitality of your second chakra. Resolving these issues will release judgment, anger, frustration, expectations, bitterness, possessiveness and many other energy-demanding emotions. You become free of the past and free of the negative energy. You must listen to your own being and nurture your emotional self. When you feel nurtured, you have the capacity to be emotionally available for others. You become more aware, present, and in the flow with the events of your everyday life.

Once you have embraced your emotions and you have expressed your repressed thoughts, you will feel relief. You have released blocked energy from your system. Along with this relief will come a sense of movement, lightness and freedom. Things may feel like they are happening a little easier, no longer holding you back. You will start living more honestly with yourself and others. At this time you will also begin to open up another level of your energy. This energy is that which allows you to create and bring to fruition your passions and ideas.

"True independence comes when we cease to force and start to flow."

Vernon Howard

Still waters run deep. When I rafted the Grand Canyon during the year of the high waters there were no rapids. There was so much water running in the Canyon that the river was very deep. The river movement was actually much slower than when the river levels were lower. Far below us were the ledges and rocks that in low water created a much faster moving environment. It is the shape and texture of the earth that creates rapids in lower water. With high water we were far from the true essence of the earth and the natural flow of the river. At high water, sitting on the boat was uneventful and I experienced the sense of barely moving. I methodically watched the canyon walls pass before me. Each day drifted by. At the time it was very relaxing but I was also disappointed. The exciting rapids I had anticipated were not there. Ultimately, we had to strap engines onto our rafts to move down river. We needed extra energy to get to our destination. Your emotions run deep and carry your passions and life purpose. If you cannot feel your emotions, it is unlikely you will be able to see in what direction you want your life to go. Your creative impulses are slowed by the lack of movement and fluidity in your life. Your river might be too full of water. Your flow may be stalled, your true essence buried.

Often, by moving yourself, you can start to identify your deepest passions and desires. Getting yourself into movement might include treating yourself to a small pleasure or allowing yourself to experience a secret desire. This allows you a few moments of natural joy. By allowing yourself this joy, you begin to incorporate greater feelings of happiness into your energy system. By exploring your feelings and emotions you understand yourself better and you become free to choose the emotions you want to feel. You consciously begin to choose to live in positive emotions, allowing yourself the right to have all the happiness you can stand. As with any type of training or developing, this takes time and practice to develop. Sometimes we actually have to practice the act of feeling good, to feel good again. Sometimes feeling good takes time and integration. The whole being must adjust to the new positive vibrations of a being that is emotionally free and open to sensing the world around them.

"We don't take pleasure serious enough."

Charles Eames

Practice the art of feeling good. Allow your being to immerse itself in the lightness of life. Practice engaging and feeling the emotions of joy, happiness and love. Each time your body experiences these powerful feelings, your body becomes more and more ready to live a radiant life. You must allow yourself to feel joy to have a joyful life. You must allow yourself to feel passion to move into expressing the passions of your life's work. You were born to be brilliant and to shine radiantly. It is up to you to develop the muscle to do so.

When you are tapped into your essential nature and your whole 'sensing' being, your brilliance and life flows. Expression comes easily and you create with less effort. You are in the boat, on the river of life, floating gracefully in the main current. Time becomes endless and the magic of life unfolds in every moment. You are free to feel and sense your inner being and the magic of the world that lies before you.

second chakra details

Element:	Water
Sanskrit:	Svadhisthana, sweetness
Color:	Orange
Location:	5th lower lumbar near the genital area
Corresponding areas:	Lower abdomen, fluids of body, bladder, kidney, sexual and reproductive areas of the body, lymphatic system
Theme:	Movement and desires, unconscious creativity
Core Shift:	I feel and have pleasure in my life experiences
Challenge:	Move through feelings of guilt

Balanced Characteristics: An individual who moves with the changes and challenges life has to offer while following their desires and passions.

Signs of Imbalance:

Too much/Expanded	*Too little/Contracted*
Overly emotional	Doesn't feel emotions
Sex addiction	Fear of pleasure
Compulsive	Needy, clinging
Overly charming	Dependent
Gets in other people's space	Possessive
Obsessive attachments	Lack of desire
Addicted to a 'rush' feeling	Often feels guilty
Emotional roller coaster	Life choices made from 'shoulds'
Overly empathic	
Poor emotional boundaries	

Physical Symptoms:

Loss of appetite for food, sex and life	Impotence
Bladder problems	Lower back pain
Disorders in the reproductive system (ovaries, testicles)	Low sex drive
	Knee problems
Problems with sexuality	Physical stiffness in the body
Prostate problems	Dry skin, lack of luster

Signs of Balance:

෴ Creative energy being expressed in life or in livelihood

෴ Easily engages with others and has good boundaries

෴ Clear sense of own feelings and emotions

෴ Easily goes with the flow of life's changes and challenges

- Experiences the pleasurable aspects of life
- Motivation based on self and values
- Empathetic (without enmeshing) with others
- Balanced expression of sexual energy and passion
- Nurturing to self and others
- Enthusiastic about life
- Is compensated with monies for creative expression and livelihood
- Feels vibrant and alive

Goal:
- Allowing, expressing, and experiencing your desires, feelings and pleasures

Activities to explore:
- Heal all past emotional wounds and addictions through 12-step programs or counseling
- Identify your top personal needs and get them met or resolved
- Develop appropriate and balanced emotional boundaries. Explore the physical sensations when your boundaries (physical and non-physical) are crossed
- Identify what you might feel guilty about and release the feelings
- Learn to embrace changes gracefully and to flow with what life presents you
- Accept your own limitations and the limitations of the people around you
- Participate in life on an emotional/sensate level
- Become self-sufficient, without being overly independent
- Develop a good sense of self-containment and a natural flow in life
- Write forgiveness letters to yourself and others (burn/destroy letters afterward)
- Explore and release any expectations you have of others
- Remove any actions or behaviors that are based on "shoulds"
- Discover desires and passions through the exploration of the inner self, felt sensations and lifelong ideal dreams. Participate in activities that honor these desires and bring them to life
- Discover when and where you lose your sense of time or experience flow

- ❧ Journal daily
- ❧ Spend time by the water: swim, go to the ocean, ride a ferry, go on a river trip, take a hot tub soak or a bath
- ❧ Participate in exercises to stimulate and balance flow movement: dancing, NIA, Kripalu yoga, boating, ice-skating
- ❧ Bodywork: Swedish massage, manual lymph drainage

shifts for the second chakra

From...	To...
"I live my life according to what I should do."	"I live a life based on my desires and passions."
"I live my life based on what is expected of me."	"I live my life based on what feels right and good for me."
"I keep my feelings and emotions to myself."	"I share my feelings and emotions with others appropriately."
"I live day-to-day numb to my potential."	"I live freely, expressing my creativity."
"I do not want to look at my 'shadow' side."	"I fully embrace all aspects of my personality, including male/female and good/bad aspects."
"I sometimes feel guilty about doing what I really want."	"I embrace what my desires are and realize the importance of expressing these qualities."
"My life is good, it is not right for me to ask for more."	"I have the right to feel and explore all desires and possibilities in my life."
"I seldom indulge myself with those extra 'feel good' things."	"I treat myself to the things that make me feel alive and good."
"My sense of feel is limited, I don't really tune into how things actually feel."	"I love touching, and feeling surfaces and textures. They are the spice of life."

Questions for journal work:

- How do you express your sexuality? How do you feel about being sexual?
- How do you respond to or react to change?
- For one full day take note of how you move. What did you discover about your movement?
- What would give you great pleasure?
- How do you relate to your emotional self?
- What desires have you never expressed?
- How well do you let others 'do' for you? Are you willing to receive unconditionally?
- When do you feel most sensual?
- What emotions do you dislike expressing? How might your life change if you became more comfortable being able to express this emotion?
- How often do you feel vibrant and alive? What would you have to believe or give up to feel this way all the time?
- What puts you in a creative flow?
- When do you lose sense of time? What are you doing?
- What makes you feel enthusiastic?
- How many of your creative ideas have come to fruition? What would need to happen for more of them to come to fruition?
- What is your secret passion that you have not taken action toward?

    ❧   What do you think everyone would think of you if you did what you truly wanted to do? Is this really true?

    ❧   If you could reinvent yourself and create something you have always wanted what might that be?

    ❧   If you had all the money in the world what would you do with it?

    ❧   Do you have any regrets in your life? Write a letter of forgiveness and release for any action you regret taking or not taking in your past.

Keywords to explore:

Desire	Flow	Emotions
Motivation	Movement	Sexuality
Creation	Pleasure	Passion
Water	Guilt	Creative seed

engaging with the energy of the second chakra

Sensing the Body

The human body carries a wealth of information and knowledge that can steer you and direct you in a manner that your intellect cannot. Your body carries your feeling body, or your emotions. Feelings and emotions are not tangible things such as the physical body. Instead the feelings and emotions held in the body are expressed on an energetic level. You sense them and feel them, although you may not see them or touch them. It is when you use both your body (the place where feelings and emotions are stored) and your intellect (your ability to direct attention and make choices) together that you can access your whole being wisdom. From this place you make decisions and take action steps that will reflect your true nature.

To first access this source of wisdom you must learn how to communicate with your body. Communicating with your body means to dialogue with your body, to engage your awareness with the sensations of the body, and to understand what the sensations are trying to convey to you. This process requires you to become very present to the subtle sensations and feelings throughout your whole body.

When you fully understand the feelings and emotions your body is trying to express, you will find you will flow and move through life with ease. It is in the second chakra that feelings and emotions are expressed and represented in the water element. Engage yourself in experiencing your emotional body so that your water element will flow with ease and you have conscious choice around how to use your emotions on your life path.

The energy body is the part of the body we cannot see, but we can feel. The emotions or feelings the body is expressing, regardless if we pay heed or not, is expressed in the energy body. Here is a simple process to begin communicating with your energy body and body wisdom:

1. Create a safe space for you to relax and engage with your body.
Find a comfortable place to sit without distractions. Turn off the television, telephone and the radio. A quiet, peaceful space will help you to more easily access your body and body wisdom. As you first begin to use this process you may need up to 20 minutes to go through the whole process. As you use the process over and over your time will decrease considerably and you will be able to communicate and access your body knowledge quickly and reliably.

2. Begin by exploring the matter at hand.

Explore the matter at hand (challenge, concern, opportunity, risk, conflict, etc.). You may want to write a few notes on a blank piece of paper. What are your concerns, fears, hesitations or conflicts? What might you be confused about? What would you like the answer to? Write your thoughts until you feel you have completed the mental process of exploring your situation.

3. Shift from a mental process to a body awareness process.

After you have completed the writing of all your concerns and questions around your challenge, conflict or item you would like to use your body wisdom to engage with, put your pen and paper down in front of you. While letting your concerns be present, breathe deeply several times and begin to let your awareness drop into your whole body.

4. Begin to dialogue with your body.

As you bring all your awareness into your body, ask yourself:

"What area of my body am I noticing the most?"

"Where does my attention go first as I begin to connect with my body?"

Sit quietly as you explore your body awareness and you identify where your attention or awareness goes in your body. Your attention may suddenly go to your stomach, the back of your neck, your back, your left leg or anywhere else in your body.

5. Identify the sensations you notice in this area of your body.

As your attention goes to a certain area of your body, take a few minutes to notice the quality of the sensations in that area. Does the area feel warm, tight, expansive, contracted, fluttering, thumping, pulsing, dull, aching, itchy etc.? Ask yourself:

"What is the feeling or sensation I am having in this area?"

"How might I describe that sensation?"

Find three or four words that help you describe the sensation.

6. Deepen your understanding of the sensation.

While keeping your attention focused on the sensations you are feeling in the identified area of your body, continue to explore the sensation further. Go deeper with your descriptions. Does this area feel congested, tight, constricted, unmoving, etc? Does the sensation remind you of a color? What are the subtle sensations within the sensation? Ask yourself:

"How else might you describe this quality?"

"What are the qualities of the sensation or feeling?"

"While you continue to observe this sensation, how else might you describe the qualities?"

7. Identify the emotional quality of the sensation.

As you explore the sensations of the feelings in your body you will now want to ask your body to help you understand what it is trying to express to you. While remaining fully engaged with the sensations you are feeling, ask yourself:

"Body, why do you have this quality, feeling or sensation?"

"Body, what is the emotion you are expressing?"

"Body, what is it you are feeling?"

Notice the first thing that bubbles up from your body. This is what your body is trying to express to you. Remember the first thought, word or insight that emerges.

Affirm the emotion identified.

Without questioning what the body is telling you, repeat out loud what you hear the body telling you.

"My body is feeling...(frustration, anger, bitterness, anxiety, stress, joy, apprehension, etc.)"

Sit with the feeling and emotion you are having and observe it inside your body for a few seconds.

8. What is the body trying to say?

Now, gently talk with your body again. Finish this sentence:

"My body is trying to tell me....

As you clearly receive the message your body is communicating to you, you may wish to return to your paper and write the message down.

9. Return to your body.

Now it is time to reconnect with the body to see what has happened to the original sensation. Bring your awareness back to your body. Ask yourself:

"Where does my attention go in my body?"

If your attention goes to the same area and you have the same sensations, you will want to explore the process again. If you have fully engaged with and communicated with the body, the sensations will mostly likely shift in quality or diminish completely. Sometimes a new sensation may be activated. Repeat the process if you feel inclined. Continue to explore the sensations within the body as they emerge with the concerns you are presently focused on.

Caveats:

⌒ Watch for any judgments or thoughts that you may experience that remove you from being present in your body. Removing judgment about the emotion behind the sensation is imperative. You are observing the sensation, feelings and emotions. Therefore judgments around 'should' or 'shouldn't' will not serve you. These thoughts bring you back up to the head. Analyzing, discounting or reasoning the feelings that emerge will also remove you from the exploration and understanding of your body's expression of inner wisdom. Focus yourself on being the observer of your own body; let it speak to you.

∾ If you find yourself going into a long answer for any of these questions, you have returned to your head. Simple one or two word answers will reflect the information your body is expressing.

∾ Answers that come very quickly, sound too precise, or are off the top of the head, are they are just that - off the top of your head. Take your time to let the words emerge and bubble up from your body.

∾ You may find yourself going into the feeling versus observing the feeling. It is your job to be the observer of your feelings. Keep yourself on the edge of the feeling, fully understanding and seeing all aspects of the feeling.

∾ You may want to check out. You may find yourself suddenly thinking about something else or falling asleep. No need to punish yourself for being distracted. Simply get yourself back on track by returning to observing your body sensations. Each time you do this the process will become easier. The first time you run three miles it feels a heck of a lot longer than the twentieth time you run three miles. This is a new technique and skill you are developing. Have patience and be kind to yourself!

∾ The chakra system is a model to use for exploration and understanding of the body mind connection. It is a very complex model and I recommend you do NOT use the model in a diagnostic manner during this process. You may want to use the model to deepen your understanding of the body mind connection and the shift that you need to make to live a richer life. If you notice patterns with the quality of your sensations and where in the body they arise, the information may help you to better understand the deeper issues you may be touching on. Most importantly, if you listen to what your body is telling you, you will find the answers you are looking for. The body does not lie to you. It is your ego and mind that may try to steer you away from the truth. Learn to distinguish the difference between body-based communications and ego-based communications.

Key Distinctions:

"Feel your feelings" vs. "Think about your feelings"

Let's face it, many of us are experts at using our heads to resolve and control aspects of our lives. Sometimes we are so good at this we ditch our intuition and our body awareness. We might at first feel our feelings and then immediately get into our head to talk about them. It is safer this way than feeling them. When this happens, there is a severe disconnection.

If your head is taking over and you are experiencing internal intellectual responses and dialogue with analogies, you will want to stop and refocus on the body. When this is happening, most often you are not feeling your feelings but thinking about them instead. When you are 'feeling,' then your sentences will shorten and you will speak in choppy English, searching for the perfect word to connect with the feeling. It might even seem difficult.

"Be 'with' feelings" vs. "Be 'in' the feelings"

When we are 'with' our feelings, we have felt them and identified what they feel like. We are right there with the sensation. It is like feeling the heat of a campfire without getting burned. We are still connected to our ability to respond to the feeling. When we are 'in' the feeling, we are basically in the campfire. We are experiencing the (burn) emotion behind the feeling. Often, if there is a high charge around the emotion, we might spiral right down into it. Then we are no longer using the body and observing; instead we are reacting and letting the emotions take over.

"Observe your feelings" vs. "Reacting to your feelings"

Again, we could use the campfire analogy. You can observe the color of the fire, the intensity of the flames and how it dances and moves without being charged up or down or affected by it. You will react to or be affected by the fire if you have not established a sense of safety or knowledge of how to interact with it. By slowly observing your body sensations, you are building a relationship with your body and learning to trust what your body is expressing. Go slowly and observe your feelings and sensations so that you are not diving into the fire.

Practice This Process

As you use this tool over and over, you change your awareness levels and increase your intuition levels. At first it may take you a while to move through the whole process. As you become more skilled and in tune with how your body wants to speak to you, the process time will become less and less. Soon you will be able to do this process in just a few short minutes. This process is all about understanding and feeling your feelings, emotions and body. To live a radiant life we must live from the inside out!

my second chakra summary

1. The insights I have about my second chakra are...

2. What I would like to focus on with regard to the second chakra is...

3. The three things I am willing to do to bring this chakra into balance and vitality are...

    1.

    2.

    3.

4. The behaviors and patterns I am willing to process, explore, release or give up are...

5. I am grateful for...

Third Chakra

Manipura

the third chakra assessment

Assess the vitality of this aspect of your life energy system. Place an "X" under the number that best represents the current status of each statement for you. Five is the highest ranking of level of truth. One represents the lowest level.

	1	2	3	4	5
People seldom, if ever, persuade me to do things that I do not want to do.			X		
I have plenty of energy and I seldom feel drained.		X			
My self-esteem is very high.		X			
I rarely find fault with or judge people.			X		
I have a strong sense of what is right and wrong and honor this level of integrity in my life.				X	
I do not take any oral substance to slow me down (e.g., alcohol, marijuana, prescription drugs).			X		
I do not consume substances that stimulate me (e.g., excessive amounts of coffee, soda, chocolate, drugs, anti-depressants).				X	
I do not experience hypoglycemia, ulcers, diabetes or digestive disorders.		X			
My stomach, pancreas, gall bladder, and liver are healthy.					
My digestion is healthy and consistent.		X			
I seldom experience frustration, anger or aggression.			X		
I assert my opinions at appropriate times.			X		
I can relax and do not rely on my adrenaline to accomplish things.				X	
I do not constantly compare or compete with others.				X	
I live a shame-free life.				X	
If I am not happy with a situation, I change my actions or thoughts to obtain different results.				X	
I do what I say I am going to do.				X	
I easily can discipline myself to take actions to reach goals.				X	
I follow through on projects I have started.				X	
I have a strong sense of purpose in my life and the action I take in life supports me in creating and living this purpose.			X		

Total of all Columns | 10 | 27 | 24 |

51

Guide for Results:

80 – 100:   Your vital energy in this chakra center is excellent at this time. Review the chapter to maintain your healthy balance.

60 – 79:   Your vital energy in this chakra center is good at this time. Take some actions to increase your possibilities and energy levels.

40 – 59:   Are you experiencing difficulties in certain areas of your life? Focus on this chakra to begin to balance and re-energize yourself.

20 – 39:   Your vital energy is zapped in this chakra. Take some action today!

0 – 19:   Yikes! Get into action now. You may want to seek professional counsel.

third chakra assessment questions

1. Which statements caught you off-guard, made you slightly uncomfortable, raised an eyebrow or caught your attention?

2. How do you feel after doing this assessment?

3. What areas of the assessment do you feel confident about?

4. What aspects of the assessment raised an emotional reaction in you? If so, what was your response?

5. What areas do you see that you might want to put some attention on releasing, healing, fixing, or creating? Please list these with three steps to support your growth in each area.

the third chakra: manipura

*T*he third chakra is the power chakra, called Manipura. The element of this chakra is fire, the color is yellow, and it is located in the solar plexus. This chakra represents our engine of personal power. The energy that lies within this chakra provides us with the source of fuel to take action and accomplish what we most desire to do in the world. To create what you would like, you must have power and will. Personal power has much to do with the quality of your relationship with yourself and with others. An individual with a healthy balanced third chakra demonstrates a balanced level of self-esteem, self-respect and personal power. When you feel powerful as a human being, this area is open, warm and full of vitality.

The third chakra provides you with the opportunity to explore how you show up in the world with your personal power and how you can use your power to create what you want. The key factor in creating vital third chakra energy is the ability to take consistent actions that are based on one's values and integrity. When what you say and what you do are congruent, you create an alignment of energy and direction. From this comes the transformation of ideas and, eventually, results.

Like the sun that burns brightly, fire can create much pleasure, such as the sensation of warmth and inner vitality. However, fire is a powerful source of energy that can easily become too powerful, or, if not cared for and attended, can easily go out. For instance, imagine the qualities you might find in a campfire. Some campfires burn in a steady fashion, bright and lovely. Other campfires require constant attention. When these fires are neglected, the flames flicker and later fade.

The fires that burn nicely have a good foundation of hot coals. A fire that burns consistently and brightly is built well and then tended to carefully. It is contained and provides warmth and light. Hot coals glow at the base of the fire and spark new materials into flame creating more heat. A fire of this nature is ready to provide more flame at anytime. It is full of potential and is actively demonstrating that potential. Conversely, when a fire is fed too much fuel it may burn out of control. This can be very destructive; destroying all that is around it. Fire produces heat that results in transformation. The way in which fire transforms depends on the foundation, the conditions and the ingredients of the fire.

Energy and vitality are key ingredients needed to take action in the world. Letting your life grow and shine is a sign of a healthy person full of vitality. Building a relationship with your fire qualities will help you establish the energy and consistency needed to stay on your life path and transform your ideas into reality. Your sense of power is primarily based on the quality of relationship you have with the self. This primary relationship then determines how you interact and how you are in relationship with others. If you are not balanced, you will feel less than or dominated by others. If you are balanced, you will have your own sense of self and know how to draw your own energy into your system. As you come to own your personal power in the world, you become more sensitive to how your actions affect other people. Establish practices that will support you in expressing your power in a balanced and caring way. Develop practices that draw your supply of power from within yourself.

Fire sparks and transforms your life. In the first chakra you focused on grounding and foundation. With the second chakra energy you explored your body sensations, feelings and emotions to find a deeper sense of yourself. In the third chakra you take the dreams and passions revealed to you in the second chakra and bring them to life through action. How you go about this determines your success. When the sun (fire) hits the earth, it heats the ground and warms the seeds beneath the soil. It is the heat from the yellow sun that cracks the shell of the seed. The fire and heat of the sun transforms the seed and calls forth growth. In the third chakra you will do the same. You call forth the ideals and values you want to base your life on and you align your actions with these principles. This will bring the sunlight to warm your life seed, crack the shell and begin the growth and transformation of your life.

What is right action? In order to make right action choices, you must first cultivate self-esteem and confidence. You must learn to listen to your inner wisdom. You must be clear about what you value and what you wish to orient your life around. This deep sense of knowing what you want and what makes you feel joy establishes the 'who' of who you really are as an individual. As you integrate the aspects of the 'who," you begin to define the actions that make you feel good and whole. Your actions are based from a heart connection. When you know what makes you feel good and whole you can listen to your 'gut' feelings and act on your intuitive messages to lead you further down the pathway that represents your values. The more you learn to trust your own instincts, the more you know your own truths. When your

"If one advances confidently in the direction of his own dreams, and endeavors to live the life which he has imagined, he will meet with a success unexpected in the common hours."

Thoreau

actions align with and support these truths, you gain your own unique personal power. You will master personal power when you are able to take actions based on what you choose to do to be in full integrity versus what you need to do to protect your unhealed emotional needs or conforming to the external pressures of society or the family structure.

Survival is about feeling safe. If you feel safer by avoiding conflict, then you might allow others to have their way in a situation in which you feel very strongly conflicted. When this happens, you may avoid expressing and taking actions that support your core beliefs in order to avoid conflict and retain harmony. You back away from a situation emotionally and energetically. Continuing to neglect your own core beliefs and thoughts diminishes your trust and ability in self-expression. Essentially you are continuing to abandon what you feel is the right course of action. You program yourself to believe that you cannot be trusted to stick up for yourself. This can result in you ignoring your own sense of integrity and replacing it with the wants and needs of others. Your self-esteem and self-worth suffer.

"Every decision you make stems from what you think you are and represents the value that you put upon yourself."

A Course in Miracles

Likewise, expressing your power by demanding that your needs and wants come before others, or ruthlessly articulating or taking immediate actions to protect your own sense of self-righteousness is also a display of unbalanced power. When this dynamic occurs you are pushing yourself onto or before others. Energetically and emotionally you are being aggressive. When you demand and take control of a situation you are most likely being driven by unfulfilled emotional needs. These actions drop you back into an unbalanced position that is reflected by unresolved second chakra issues. You appear, not powerful, but aggressive, controlling and dominating.

Think of the fires of the western United States. Old growth forested areas often become a fire hazard. These forests can easily ignite into infernos, raging out of control, destroying everything in their paths. In the end, there is nothing left unchanged. All is destroyed. This natural process sweeps clean the environment of everything. The next spring life begins to return and the forest begins rebuilding. Although it is a natural cycle in nature, the energy of fire can have dramatic and extreme results. This type of old growth forest fire can be likened to a person who has a repressed sense of personal power. Repressed feelings and actions are like the fires that rage in the old growth forest. At some point this repressed sense of power is vulnerable to igniting and creating a situation that swings to the far extreme, burning and destroying with anger, rage and resentment. Basing your actions on your integrity, what is right for you, all day, everyday, keeps your fire energy vital and potent, burning slowly and consistently, versus out of control.

Keeping the forest fire example in mind, take a look at your life. Does it resemble the old forest growth that has not experienced any flames? Are you vulnerable to sparks? Do you sometimes have thoughts, feelings and emotions that you have not expressed? Do you lack the clarity and action needed to create what you want? Or, are you burning out of control, constantly demanding and pushing for your own way? When you are not clear about what works for you or what feels right for you, life carries you in random directions. You often react quickly, far from being centered in your being. If you continue to live this way you eventually experience major and extreme events that "wake you up." These wake up experiences are your forest fire(s). You may wake up one day and realize that you are living a life you really don't like. You might become angry, full of fire, wanting a life change. Whether planned or not, these major life shifts that emerge can look like job changes, major health problems, major accidents, loss of job, loss of home, or a divorce.

The first crucial step to increase your personal power is to restore the integrity of your life and being so that you sustain a warm glowing energy that provides you with the clarity and vitality to achieve what you want in the world. Your integrity is different from every other person's integrity on the earth. It is an individual experience that can only be defined for one's self. Another person cannot tell you what defines your integrity. This can only come from within you as you contact the sensation and feeling you have when you know you are doing what is right.

Integrity is what feels like "right action" for you at any given time in your life. Integrity is defined by right actions taken that are aligned with your beliefs about what you believe to be right and what you believe to be wrong. Your integrity will reflect what is most important to you, your personal values and your morals. When you are living with integrity you feel good about who you are and what you are doing. This increases your life energy and provides ample energy to go beyond surviving to thriving.

Everyone has a different opinion about what is right and wrong regardless if it is about lying, lateness, stealing, adultery, gossiping, littering, hurting others, murder, or war. Increase your awareness around what are wrong or right actions for yourself and you will begin to shift your perspective and your behaviors. Challenge what society defines as acceptable and reach into the core of your being and define what is acceptable from that place. As you change your beliefs and behaviors, you raise your standards and you make new choices. As you develop this deeper relationship with yourself and hold yourself accountable for your actions—all actions, small and big—you become a more and more powerful person. You learn that you can trust yourself to take the actions that honor the deepest part of you.

"Integrity means to be whole and undivided—to be authentic—as when our true heart speaks through our thoughts, words, and actions. If our experience of inner truth is not made real through our actions, we will lose the power of authenticity and feel the twinge of self-betrayal."

Rob Rabbin

"Power is standing strongly in your own center and living from your heart."

Sark

Consider the following three scenarios:

Person 'A' stays at a beautiful hotel and falls in love with the luscious towels and decides to keep one. When arriving at home, she hangs the towel in the bathroom and does not give the action she took to acquire the towel much thought. This person is in integrity since there are no feelings of 'less-than' by having taken the towel home.

Person 'B' takes the towel home and then later regrets it. Due to this person's guilty feelings, the towel is either kept hidden or thrown away. This person is out of integrity since there are feelings of shame and regret, without right action.

Person 'C' gets home from a trip to discover that the hotel towel is in a suitcase. Knowing that the towel belongs to the hotel, this person takes one of two actions: calls the hotel apologizing for this action, offering to pay for the towel or puts the towel into the mail, sending it back to the hotel with a note of apology. This person is in integrity since action was taken to rectify a situation that was viewed as not 'right' for them. This person feels good about himself and the action taken to rectify the situation.

"My philosophy is that not only are you responsible for your life, but doing the best at this moment puts you in the best place for the next moment."

Oprah Winfrey

Both person 'A' and person 'C' are in their integrity. They feel right about their actions. Person 'B' feels wrong about what was done, and therefore is out of integrity.

The difference between person 'A' and 'C' is that person 'A' might be viewed as having a low level of personal integrity and power. One might view person 'A' as being thoughtless about the actions taken. This observation implies that person 'A' has a lower sense of self-responsibility. Person 'B' might be viewed as having a higher level of integrity than person 'A' since there are feelings of regret; however, there is a lack of personal power since some form of 'right action' was not taken.

Person 'C' might be viewed as having the highest level of integrity as there is a clear sense of moral responsibility, of what is right or wrong, along with specific actions taken in accordance to the rules established for himself. Person 'C' has the highest level of personal power (thus more vital energy) and, in the long run, will (theoretically) not only outlast the other two, but will have more energy in moving forward in life. Person 'C' has clarity and acts according to that clarity. Person 'C' demonstrates a powerful way to live life.

You may not agree with the actions that person 'A' took. In fact, you could judge the level of integrity for each of these individuals. How you judge them will solely depend on your current level of integrity — what you value along with the level of responsibility you take for your own actions.

The bottom line is that increasing your awareness about how the actions you take in your life have you feel (i.e. good or bad, guilty or proud, etc.) will increase your awareness of your own integrity level. This awareness will directly affect your level of personal power, as you will make more aligned and effective choices based upon it. This is important groundwork for creating your own personal power. It dictates how your own natural force shows up in the world.

How do you build a clear and strong relationship with yourself about what is right and wrong action? Vague ideas about what is right and wrong leaves you with a weak relationship with yourself resulting in lower self-esteem and self-respect. Being vague keeps you in a place of being unable to make a decision and ultimately move in any direction. Being vague lets you off the hook of responsibility. Being vague is being powerless. Challenge yourself to move into a more powerful position by questioning many things that you have either taken for granted or simply not given thought to. Ask yourself: How do I want to be in the world? How do I want to be perceived? Do my actions reflect what I truly value? Do I feel good about the actions I take on a daily basis? How do I act and how do my actions serve, or not, serve me?

With the first chakra, you explored the physical aspect of your being. In the second chakra, you focused on the emotional aspects. Here in the third chakra, the energy is governed by mental activity. What you think mentally leads you into action. This is why you must be clear about what you value. You also must be very clear and precise about the thoughts that you entertain in your head. These thoughts are what lead into action or into non-action. Your thoughts are the primary relationship to yourself with your self. Your thoughts program you on your attitude about your body, mind and spirit. If you spend any of your time beating yourself up for what you have not done, how poorly you did what you did do, or how stupid, unreliable, incompetent, or unworthy a person you are, your actions or non-actions will reflect these very thoughts. You actions will lack authenticity, integrity and personal power. You must fine tune your mental thoughts and create thoughts that honor your being and raise your sense of self and confidence. Self-esteem, self-respect, self-discipline and self-confidence all have one thing in common. These words are 'self' based words. You must embody the energy of these words in your own being, your own self, in order to be able to take the actions that support you on your life path. To do this you must learn to control your own mind and to increase the thoughts that are positive and fill you with a higher sense of self and

"The ancestor of every action is thought."

Ralph Waldo Emerson

purpose. You must start with what is going on inside of your mind before you can shift your outer life.

You may also use your body in the process of deepening your sense of personal power and self. The third chakra is located in the upper digestive area of the body near the solar plexus. It is here that your body first digests all that you consume in the way of foods and nutrients. When you eat things that do not agree with your system, your body tells you. You get a stomachache, feel bloated or sometimes your body completely rejects what you have consumed and you become sick. Your body knows what is right and what is not appropriate. The third chakra is also where you digest the activities of life. Your third chakra will tell you what appropriate action is. You must learn to communicate and listen to it.

Before you take any action, try exploring your felt sensations. What is the sense you get in your body about your decisions? When you fail to listen to the messages of wisdom from your body, you often react, versus respond, to a situation and then regret the actions that follow. By reacting in a different manner than what is congruent to your whole body, you split your energy being. In these situations you create an internal conflict that removes from and drains you of your personal power.

"You must feel who you really are, then, do what you need to do, in order to have what you want."

Margaret Young

The key piece is understanding and knowing, from a physical sensation or experience, what works best for you and honors your being. This feeling-based sensation allows you to identify situations that are not right for you by being aware of your physical experience. You learn to trust your 'gut' feeling. Think of a time when you had a gut feeling that clearly told you what right action was, and instead of acting on this gut feeling, you allowed something else to transpire. The result was that you felt bad about the situation and your part in it. The lack of right action most likely affected your level of integrity and self-esteem. Essentially, you experienced that you could not rely on yourself to listen to yourself. That is an enormous disconnection from personal power. When you listen to the knowledge in your body, and you act accordingly, your sense of self and personal power expands and grows effortlessly.

What is it really that you are listening for when you listen to your felt sensations? There are many things you could listen for and be aware of in your body. For instance, you could listen for an internal shift of your presence or an internal shift in your energy. You could listen for the funny feeling in your stomach, a gut feeling, a "hit" or "vibe." You could listen for other body responses such as the tightening or raising of shoulders, or the contraction in your chest. You could listen for when you just plain do not feel good about something. The key is to listen deeply to your inner being and feel the messages from your body. Use these messages as a guide to keep your whole being congruent with your actions.

Once you have established a strong sense of what is right action for yourself you must also act accordingly. You must learn how to continue to propel yourself forward increasing your momentum with every right action. You may have to embrace courage and take risks. You may feel fear. Because you are very clear about what you do feel in your body, you will be able to distinguish between fear and the gut feeling that says to avoid action. Fear can be a powerful source of energy to tap into. Be present with the feeling of fear. If you know and calculate the risks you take when you engage with any action, you have awareness. Educate yourself on the consequences of your actions. You must also be willing to take full responsibility for those actions. Feel the fear and take the action. One step of action will clarify your next step and direction. Clarity gives us more power. Movement aligned with clarity brings transformation.

"It's all right to have butterflies in your stomach. Just get them to fly in formation."

Dr. Ron Gilbert

Regardless of what you might be trying to create in your life, if you cannot continue to take action toward that goal or vision, you will not attain it. Your fire will go out. There will be no energy left. Momentum builds more energy. Fires need more wood to continue to burn. When you feed your fire the best wood, wood that is perfectly matched to burn in the fire, you create more fire. Imagine each step to be fuel for your fire. Each of your action steps must be aligned with your integrity; thus providing the best fuel. You must feel good about how you are going about your business and your life.

Taking right actions that are based on your values will provide you a strong sense of self: self-esteem, self-confidence, self-respect, and self-reliance. The strengthening and balancing of your personal power will support you in the growth of your life and relationships. A healthy third chakra center is about your ability to take actions that are based on knowing yourself well. Tend to your own personal fire. Let it warm and crack the seed of your life purpose. Be sure it burns brightly without bringing harm to anyone else. Let your fire keep perfect warm coals that will spark with more fuel and not rage out of control. Distinguish the best fuel for your fire and your life. Make good choices for yourself. When a choice feels like it wasn't the best, simply make a new one based upon the clarity of what feels right. Shift your thoughts to the positive aspects of the learning you are experiencing on your path. Continue taking right actions — build your momentum. Watch as your life transforms.

third chakra details

Element:	Fire
Sanskrit:	Manipura, Lustrous gem
Color:	Yellow
Location:	Solar plexus (between navel and base of sternum)
Corresponding areas:	Muscular system, digestive system (liver and small intestines), muscles, gall bladder, pancreas, endocrine glands
Theme:	Personal power
Core Shift:	I am a powerful individual whose actions reflect a deep sense of inner worth
Challenge:	Overcome shame and embrace the courage to take risks

Balanced Characteristics:

An individual who demonstrates a high level of self esteem, self respect, purpose and the ability to move forward and out into the world while having a high level of awareness and consideration of those around them.

Signs of Imbalance:

Too much/Expanding	*Too little/Constricting*
Blaming	Weak will
Resentful	Low self-esteem
Explosive	Passive
Controlling others	Apathetic
Comparing/judging of others	Sluggish
Aggressive	Beats self up (negative thoughts of self)
Scattered	Controlled by others
Constantly active	Low energy
Dominating	Fearful to take risks

Physical Symptoms:

Stomach ulcers	Hypertension
Chronic fatigue	Disorders with gallbladder and liver
Weight around middle of body	Digestive problems
Diabetes (pancreas)	Pain in the mid to lower back
Allergies	

Signs of Balance:

- Perceived as warm and inviting to others

- Responsible with thoughts, words and actions

- High level of integrity - knows what is right and wrong for self

- Is respectful to self and others

- Is own source of worth and esteem
- Interacts with others respectfully and gracefully
- Sees others as being their best
- Measures self only with self (doesn't compare)
- Movement and actions are based on life purpose, goals and values
- Ability to follow through on commitments and projects
- Able to take calculated risks - understands consequences
- Has mastered self through mind
- Expresses vitality and spontaneity

Goal:
- To consistently take actions that are based on your integrity, self esteem, and self respect

Activities to explore:
- Develop a strong sense of self-esteem
- Explore the meaning of integrity; identify when you are out of integrity. Raise your standards. Take actions that put you into your integrity
- Tap into your physical vitality through exercise. (Determine what sparks you)
- Practice exercises for spontaneity (letting go of control and risk taking)
- Establishing a physical posture that reflects the embodiment of personal power and self worth
- Develop life/work purpose statements
- Establish goals, the steps to achieve them and maintain action toward achieving them
- Deepen understanding of self on all levels
- Shift to language that supports personal power
- Release anger and shame issues
- Get complete with everything you wished you had done in your life
- Journal daily about actions you have taken and goals you are focusing on
- Use meditation to explore your internal energy system
- Notice in your body when you are 'fired up' or 'charged down'
- Observe how you feel before, during and after interacting with others

→ Participate in exercises to stimulate and balance powerful movements: alpine skiing, kickboxing, sport climbing, aerobics, martial arts, asthanga or Bikram yoga

→ Bodywork: Rolfing, myo-facial release, energy-based therapy, Feldenkrist, acupuncture, Alexander Method

shifts for the third chakra

From...	To...
"It bothers me when I don't feel like I can control a situation."	"I know I can't always control a situation but I can control my thoughts and actions with regard to the situation."
"I let others decide for me."	"I make decisions based on my needs and wants."
"I react to events that happen around me."	"I know what steps and actions I need to take to live in my integrity."
"I am often resentful or blaming of myself or others."	"I have a strong sense of purpose and act on this."
"I am apathetic, fearful and often passive in conversations and decision-making processes."	"I am energized, courageous and graceful in my actions, speech and decisions."
"I have no idea what to do with myself."	"I have a purpose that excites me and propels me forward."
"I constantly feel low energy."	"I feel alive and energized everyday."
"Sometimes I run people over with my drive and ambition."	"People are energized by my energy and love to be near me."
"My power scares me so I try to be more submissive and nice."	"I know the appropriate use of my personal power and can apply it without harming others."
"I have no stamina...it should be easier...I don't know how I'm going to keep up."	"Things often take time to come to fruition and I have the endurance to stay with the project, idea and/or vision."
"It's my way or the highway."	"Let's take everything into consideration."
"I often feel meek and intimidated by people of authority."	"I have no problem making requests and stating my opinions to people in authority."
"I am pretty casual, I don't always follow through with commitments, who does these days?"	"I am good for my word. I do what I say I am going to do."
"Life seems like such a chore, I can't motivate to get my life together."	"Each day I take a step towards the life I want to create."
"I sometimes get down on myself or mentally beat myself up for not doing or saying the right things."	"I know the power of thought and of the mind. I can control my thoughts to create positive life flow."
"I really should do _____."	" I want and will do what feels best and right for me."

Questions for journal work:

- What does power mean for you?
- When do you feel most powerful in your life?
- When do you feel the least powerful in your life? How do you think people perceive you (warm, cool, cold, glowing, hot, fiery)?
- What is the motivation behind your actions?
- Think of someone you know and respect whom you also view as powerful. List the qualities that best describe them.
- What do you need to do to embrace these qualities?
- What are the abuses of power you have observed in your life?
- Review the last two questions. How do you also express these qualities?
- What do you currently "not" want in your life? Please make a list. After each item list two action steps you can take to eliminate these things.
- What does the word integrity mean to you?
- How do you know when you have stepped out of your integrity?
- When do you most often fail to act on your gut feeling?
- What would you have to shift in your beliefs to feel a sense of balanced power?
- What thoughts do you entertain that keep you small?
- What builds your sense of self-confidence?
- Please list three goals that you have had for longer than two years. For each of these goals, please answer the following:
  - What is stopping me from reaching this goal?
  - What part of this goal is hardest to achieve?
  - What is blocking your will or ability to achieve this goal?
  - What are your choices with regard to your goals?
  - What actions will you take to accomplish the goal?
  - How will you know when you have results?

Keywords:

Fire	Power	Energy levels
Spark	Vitality	Will
Control	Authority	Warmth
Hot	Transformation	Thought to matter
Integrity	Digestion	Actions toward purpose

engaging with the fire energy

To have power does not mean to overpower others. To have personal power means that you embody our own power, energy and vitality. It is inside of you. To be a powerful person means that you have your own source of energy and will to create and take action based on what feels right for you, from conscious choice. Personal power is derived from an internal source of energy, not from an external source. The internal source of energy is tapped into and enriched when you take consistent actions that align with what you say you are going to do, and what you believe is the best thing to do.

The posture of your body expresses how powerful you feel. There is a big difference between someone who stands erect with shoulders square, chin level, and eyes forward, and a person who slouches over, shoulders rounded, stomach folded, chin and eyes slightly downward or to the side. An individual will naturally give a person with a powerful erect posture more credibility than one who is slouched over. Sometimes if this erect posture is too rigid, the power held within the person may be unyielding or unbending. This person then becomes overpowering versus empowering. Remember the bully in the schoolyard? What was the essence of his/her posture? A balanced power position allows an individual to draw on his or her own source of energy to make good decisions and to take right action, at no cost to others.

The Power Posture

Consider your own posture. As you stand, notice your body. What do you feel in your legs, hips, torso, shoulders, neck and head? Simply observe, without judgement, your normal, day-to-day stance. Close your eyes and observe what happens. Where do you sense your energy? What happens to your balance? What does your body want to do as you stand with your eyes closed? Simply take note and observe.

Now, bring your awareness into your legs and feet. Focus your intention that they are firmly planted on the ground. Feel a solid connection. Bring your awareness up into your hips, rotate your hips, front to back and side to side until you find a solid position that feels congruent and connected to your feet and legs. Bringing your awareness to your torso and back, lengthen your torso and stretch your posture as if you are actually growing taller. Imagine a string attached to your head, gently pulling you upward, creating space between each of the vertebrae in your spinal column. Move and lift a few times until you feel your height has grown a bit. Close your eyes and observe your body. Where does your attention go? Where do you feel tingles, openings, release, space and new energy?

Bring your attention to your chest. Lift your chest slightly, pushing the center of your chest slightly upward and outward, your shoulders may want to shift slightly to the back and down just slightly, notice this shift. Take a few deep breaths as you notice the shifts in your energy levels. Now notice your head and face. Face forward, your chin is parallel to the floor, eyes are gazed forward. Take a few more deep breaths. Feel the subtle shifts in your body as you experiment with this new posture. While maintaining the length in your back, let your weight settle into your feet and legs establishing good grounding.

Place your hands, one over the other, on your belly. Slowly begin to massage your belly and solar plexus area. Always move from the lower right, to the upper right, to the center, then to the upper left area, down to the lower left area and around again, in a circular pattern. Breathe deeply as you move your hands slowly around, gently pressing and massaging your belly and stomach, make a slight hissing sound as you release your breath. Move around your stomach, two to three times. Place your hands on your solar plexus. Breathe in and out, bring your attention into your legs and feet as you remain grounded. Let your hands come to your sides. Embody the energy of action and power coming from deep within your body, fully grounded. Fine tune your power posture until it feels natural, resourceful and full of vital energy.

Bring your attention into your body. Where does your attention go in your body? What sensations do you feel in this area? Bring your attention to your third chakra area. What do you feel there? Do you feel grounded, yet ready to engage and take action? Do you feel centered and congruent in your whole being?

Practice and establish your power posture often. This posture will help you to feel more confident and connected to your inner core, with your solar plexus engaged in a relaxed yet strong manner. Pay attention to when you feel congruent in your body and in your stance. Practice this powerful-feeling posture throughout the day. How does it affect your mental activity? Do you think more positive, proactive, confident thoughts? Implement this posture when you are lacking energy or the ability to take action. Does it shift your mental perspective, thus your ability?

Implement your power posture as often as possible. Stand tall and strong, fully aware of the energy and potential you hold inside. Remember this is not a posture to overpower others. It is a posture to embrace your own powerful being from the inside out. It is a posture to help you stay centered and in your core of being. Use your body as a guide to increase your awareness of the feeling of being a powerful person drawing on your own instinct and sense of right action. Set your intention to bring more and more of this feeling into your being. Keep your awareness on how this changes your life. See what shapes and moves in your external world.

Notice your posture when you are interacting with others. Sometimes you can naturally lose your sense of personal power without even realizing it. Use this technique to increase your awareness of how your personal sense of power shifts around others. Now, imagine that all around your body there is an invisible veil of energy shaped like an egg. Imagine the edge of this egg to be about two feet from your body. This is your vital energy emanating from your physical body. As you stand in your power posture imagine this invisible egg to be a wonderful glowing sunny color. You exude this wonderful, powerful vital energy. Breathe deeply into your body, imagining each breath creating more and more vitality in your energy field. You are connected to the life force inside yourself and all around your being.

As you go out into the world, pay attention to how you feel as you interact with others. Imagine how this sunny bright energy mingles with others. Does your energy invite others to become powerful beings with you? Or, does your energy want to over take others, pushing yourself onto them, moving forward aggressively? When you are with others, do you want to shrink away and become small? Notice how you feel before, during and after talking with others. How does your physical body respond and how does your energy body respond?

Powerful people embody their vitality and energy in the physical body and also in their energetic body; the part of the body that surrounds us that many of us cannot see, but can sense. Powerful people have an abundance of energy and are not dependent on others to feel good about who they are and what they are doing. Instead, they exude the desire to see others in their own personal power. A powerful person invites others to step into their own greatness and power without feelings of fear or scarcity. A powerful person looks for the gem in every other person, and this act in itself empowers others to move closer to their own greatness. A powerful person stands tall as an individual, while inviting others to engage their own power to create something better for all.

Take time this week to notice how you hold your physical body. Consider what shifts you might incorporate to embody your own powerful energy. Also notice what happens with your energy field, on the slightest of levels, as you engage with others. Bring your awareness into your body and your energy field; observe how your powerful energy dances within yourself and with others. You are the source of your magnificence and vitality!

my third chakra summary

1. The insights I have about my third chakra are...

2. What I would like to focus on with regard to the third chakra is...

3. The three things I am willing to do to bring this chakra into balance and vitality are...

    1.

    2.

    3.

4. The behaviors and patterns I am willing to process, explore, release or give up are...

5. I am grateful for...

Fourth Chakra

Anahata

the fourth chakra assessment

Assess the vitality of this aspect of your life energy system. Place an "X" under the number that best represents the current status of each statement for you. Five is the highest ranking of level of truth. One represents the lowest level.

	1	2	3	4	5
I love all aspects of myself.					
I seldom experience stress. I am content with my life.					
My immune system is healthy.					
When I give to others, I do not expect a certain response.					
I do not judge or find fault in others; I accept them as they are.					
I seldom feel lonely or isolated.					
I sleep under eight hours per night.					
I do not watch more than five hours of television per week.					
I easily can receive warmth, love and kindness that others give me.					
When someone pays me a compliment, I say "thank you."					
I have fully grieved the loss of people I have loved.					
I forgive others that have hurt or offended me.					
My heart, lungs, thymus, breasts, and arms are healthy and pain-free.					
I have healed the wounds of my inner child.					
People are more important to me than things or results.					
I let others love me and reflect back my greatness.					
I acknowledge others for who they are, not what they have.					
I know how I am of service to others, humanity or the environment.					
I embrace both the painful and joyful experiences life offers me.					
I am patient with myself and others.					

Total of all Columns

Guide for Results:

80 – 100:	Your vital energy in this chakra center is excellent at this time. Review the chapter to maintain your healthy balance.
60 – 79:	Your vital energy in this chakra center is good at this time. Take some actions to increase your possibilities and energy levels.
40 – 59:	Are you experiencing difficulties in certain areas of your life? Focus on this chakra to begin to balance and re-energize yourself.
20 – 39:	Your vital energy is zapped in this chakra. Take some action today!
0 – 19:	Yikes! Get into action now. You may want to seek professional counsel.

fourth chakra assessment questions

1. Which statements caught you off-guard, made you slightly uncomfortable, raised an eyebrow or caught your attention?

2. How do you feel after doing this assessment?

3. What areas of the assessment do you feel confident about?

4. What aspects of the assessment raised an emotional reaction in you? If so, what was your response?

5. What areas do you see that you might want to put some attention on releasing, healing, fixing, or creating? Please list these with three steps to support your growth in each area.

the fourth chakra: anahata

he fourth chakra is the heart chakra, called Anahata. The fourth chakra bridges us from the more grounded energies of survival needs, desires, and personal power represented in the lower chakras, to the fifth through seventh chakras, which represent a higher level of choice, spiritual awareness, and the energetic subtleties of life. The energy of the first chakra helped you to create a feeling of connection, abundance, and solid relationship with your body. The second chakra focused on being more in touch with your emotional body and allowing yourself to fully engage with your lifelong passions and desires. The third chakra helped you to align yourself with your integrity, expanding your capacity for self-esteem and personal power. The fourth chakra is the chakra of loving and connecting energy. It is here that less visible and less tangible qualities of energy begin to emerge as one begins to connect deeper and deeper to the self and to others.

Green is the color for the fourth chakra and represents the transformational healing powers of the heart chakra. This chakra provides the opportunity to explore your ability to have loving thoughts and feelings toward yourself and others, regardless of the exterior circumstances. A person with a balanced, open, healthy fourth chakra is accepting and compassionate with others and with the self. A vibrant fourth chakra energy flows out into the world, feeling the infinity of connection and oneness with the world. In this way, love becomes the glue that holds all living beings together. Without love there is no connection, understanding or relating. When love is present a person is in relationship to other people, other cultures and the environment. The act of loving opens one to all people, animals and aspects of the world.

The fourth chakra element is air. Air can be soft, gentle, light, and flowing. It can also be persistent, harsh, cold, and relentless. It is forever changing and moving. Air sometimes changes quickly with no warning and, at other times, there is a gradual building or shifting. Air touches everything. If you live on this earth you cannot escape air, nor can you live without it. It is there whether you are thinking about it or not. It feeds your body fresh oxygen so that you may grow and thrive. Air brings forth the change of seasons and climates. The winds in the world carry the pollens of plants and trees in the environment.

"And now here is my secret, a very simple secret; It is only with the heart that one can see rightly; What is essential is invisible to the eye."

(The fox in
The Little Prince)
Antoine De
Saint-Exupery

Air, just like love, is everywhere. It is the glue that bonds everything that is alive on earth. You cannot live without air, and a life without love is hardly worth living. You cannot see air. You must train yourself to feel the subtleties of air. Love is similar. The many levels and subtleties of love are all around, you. The energy of love is available to you at all times. When love is present, life expands. Love provides you the opportunity to live a richer life filled with sweetness and connection to others and spirit. To live life engaged with the fourth chakra energy is to live life centered in the heart.

One can begin to engage with the heart energy by observing how one balances the flow and experiences of life. Just as one takes in air into the body, one also takes in life into their being and heart. Take a moment to bring your awareness into your chest area. Follow the flow of air in and out of your lungs and chest. Notice any sensations in your chest or heart as you bring your breath into your being and as you let that breath flow back out. You may want to experiment with increasing the depth of your breath, moving more and more air deeper into your lungs, expanding your stomach for the inhale and pulling it in for the exhale. Notice how well you are able to move and stay with the observation of your own breath. What is the quality of your breath? Do you breathe deeply into your belly and lungs? Or is your breath shallow, quick, or short, filling only your upper lung area? Observe what happens to your breath when you are a faced with fear, judgment and sharp words. Conversely, what happens to your chest, lungs and heart when you experience joy, kind words, compliments, and friendship? How do you feel when these negative and positive qualities are present in your life? Notice how it is when you start, then notice how it might have shifted at the end of five minutes.

How you breathe may represent how well you are able to move in your life. The breath represents one's ability to take in and let go of the experiences life brings, regardless of the exterior circumstances. When a person is stressed, feeling hurt or pain, the breath will shift. It may become shallow, weak, or constricted. When a person is filled with joy and acceptance of the self and others, there is no resistance and the breath moves freely in a state of expansion. Love leads us to sensations of expansion. The lack of love brings you into a contracted state or a place of limited movement on an energetic level. A contracted state prevents you from being open and receptive to life experiences. The challenge for the fourth chakra is to learn how to maintain an open and compassionate energy state at all times in life, during both the painful and the joyful moments.

The main learning with this chakra is to live a life based on love, kindness and compassion. It means to live life with an open heart, through the good

"Everything in life responds to the song of the heart."

Earnest Holmes

"The essence of our spiritual being is goodness, compassion, forgiveness, love and a life of service."

Jaya Sarada,
The Path of Return

times and through the bad times. To live with love means to gracefully embrace and willingly explore the transitions, challenges and gifts that shape one's life. To have an open heart is to love others. More importantly, is also means to let the love of others into your own heart. There must be a two-way flow to achieve balance. There is a constant experience of both giving and receiving.

To experience pain is to be alive. Like all other muscles, when the heart is pushed to its limits, one may experience pain. This pain often reminds us of how alive we really are. As with any other muscle, the heart needs to be used and exercised to maintain vitality and health. The act of 'being with' what is in life, even when it is painful, allows the heart muscle to fully express itself, flexing and stretching its tissue, developing strength. The goal is not to create only happy feelings and to ignore other feelings such as sadness or hurt. The key element is to be able to be with all feelings. This means we must observe them, feel the sensations that are a part of them, and let the sensations and feelings move through the heart muscle. When this is done, the feeling is expressed, the heart responds and then the energy around the heart dissipates and the heart relaxes again. Conversely, when feelings are held in, the energy becomes frozen. The heart is contracted and restricted. The natural movement and flow of the heart's muscle is disrupted and the movement of life is slowed or stopped. The lungs struggle to breathe in air deeply and naturally and the whole body suffers.

What makes the heart contract? Any feelings or thoughts that reject aspects of life are contracting energies. Contracting feelings and thoughts include perspectives that hold one's quality of being as less than or diminished. Focusing on negative aspects, or resisting qualities or character traits in others also contracts the heart energy. Thoughts and feelings of this nature pull life force energy inward and ultimately creates separation with others and with the environment. Contracting feelings and behaviors include holding grudges, bitterness, jealously, judging or being critical of the self or others, envy, and resentment. When these feelings and thoughts are projected outward at others, or when you project them on or at yourself, you are creating more of the same contracting energy. Thus, you are separating yourself from others or yourself. The message behind all these emotions is that the situation is not acceptable. When you enter into these emotions you enter into resistance. Thus, the inward and outward flow of energy has slowed or stopped. The connecting energy of the heart is diminished. An invisible wall goes up. The bottom line is you have separated yourself from others. Acceptance and compassion opens the door back up so that life, and the heart energy, can flow again.

" If you judge people you have no time to love them."

Mother Teresa

"My religion is very simple, my religion is kindness."

Dalai Lama

Humans seek connection and love. Connection and love allows people to see the reflection of their own being, values and uniqueness in the world. Even when people are driven to achieve more money, power, recognition, or sex, the primary driving force is a need for connection, love, reflection and validation. The basis of love starts from within the self and not from others. It is every individual's responsibility to learn the art of self love: not a love that is self-ish or self-less, but a love that is based on self-ness, a love that reflects a deep connection to one's own heart. Yet it is often the most difficult thing for people to give themselves. Western society is programmed to seek exterior achievements and acquire things to obtain the experience of inner happiness, feelings of connection, worth, and love. These external events seldom, if ever, fulfill the calling of the heart. Unfortunately, for many individuals, years may pass before this realization is made.

When a person is unconsciously trying to fill the needs of unbalanced lower chakras, most likely one will be leading a life that is driven by the needs of the ego. The ego is mainly concerned with the individual. In the third chakra the energy of personal power is balanced through right actions and control of the mental activity. The ego is seen for what it is, fear-based thoughts that create separation. A heightened awareness around mental thoughts and activities supports a person in moving away from being controlled by ego-based thoughts into heart-based thoughts. Heart-based thoughts are grounded in love and openness to connection. The focus broadens from an 'I' based attitude to a "we" based perspective. The more and more one can move into the place of connecting with the heart, the easier it becomes to create a life based on one's values and joy. The perspective shifts from 'what I do and what I have is who I am', to 'this is who I am and how I serve.' The process of understanding how all life is interconnected in spirit and energy shifts one's perspective and life concerns to a broader more humanitarian based sense of livelihood and purpose. The heart wants love, connection and joy for all.

Energies that allow movement and connection are found in practicing compassion, acceptance, kindness and forgiveness. All of these energies must be integrated in the self before being directed at others. Compassion and acceptance begs one to dig deeper to fully understand what it means to be a human being. These qualities require you to embrace not only what you want to look at, but also those less desirable qualities you would rather ignore (your shadow). When a person cannot accept their own aspects and characteristics, they can not accept the same aspects in others (regardless if the aspects and characteristics are positive or negative). A wall goes up and separation is formed. As a person comes to accept the self, shortcomings and all, they see and understand all of humanity on a different level. They see themselves in others. They do not see or experience separation. There is no

"Do all the good you can, in all of the ways you can, to all the souls you can, in every place you can, at all the times you can, with all the zeal you can, as long as ever you can."

John Wesley

discomfort or judgment with what one sees in others because one has seen it, and still sees it, and accepts it already within the self. You can have compassion and acceptance because you have lifted the judgment from your own being. Kindness flows and the heart energy grows stronger.

You cannot see in others that which you do not have in yourself. As you admire others, pay attention to what it is you admire. Remember you have that same capacity and energy within yourself. Let that energy flow through and be expressed in your being. In this way you increase your connection and love with yourself.

The exploration and healing of your shadow self, all that you would rather not look at, can be a humbling experience. Self-examination gives us personal power. We begin to distinguish what we want versus what our ego is projecting. Once the ego is released, then there is no fear; the only thing left is love. In this way the fourth chakra bridges the gap between the earthy and ego-driven needs of the first three chakras to the spiritual and expansive qualities of the fifth, sixth, and seventh chakras, which leads one to liberation. When you fully feel love, you feel fully connected to yourself, others and the universal energy. It is your pivotal point for many layers and dimensions of integration.

Forgiveness keeps the energy of the heart flowing. When forgiveness is not present, acceptance has also gone by the wayside. When you forgive another, you have made a choice to break the energetic bonds of debt, or at least your perceived interpretation of debt. When you carry a grudge or judgment you also carry the energy of that feeling and thought. Your grudge or judgment affects your energy, not the person you hold the feeling against. To enter into forgiveness you must leave behind the ego's need to be right. The ego wants desperately to be right. If the ego is right it can continue to manipulate and control your thoughts, emotions and ultimately your perception of reality. Embracing the choice to live versus to be right brings you to the present moment with an open awareness. The ego has no power to resist and you are back into the flow of life; you embrace the ability to be present with exactly what is. When you forgive, a weight is lifted, reflecting to you how much of a load you have been carrying within yourself. You discover that you are the one that is losing vital life energy by holding a negative perspective or feeling toward someone else.

Embracing self-acceptance and love is a powerful act that brings vital energy into your fourth chakra. It is only when you master this that you can transfer the same treatment and energy to others. If you try to accept others before you have accepted yourself, then more of your energy is going to others instead of to you. This creates an unbalanced energy flow. You are trying to

"The ultimate lesson all of us have to learn is unconditional love, which includes not only others but ourselves as well."

Elisabeth Kubler-Ross

"To forgive is the highest, most beautiful form of love. In return, you will receive untold peace and happiness."

Robert Muller

give more to the world and others than to your self. This causes a conflicting flow of energy between the outside world, your relationship with yourself, and your relationship with spirit. When you put your energy out to others before taking care of yourself, you leak out your vital life force. By working through the issues explored in the first three chakras, one is more prepared to live a life based on a heart connection. You learn to be the source of your own energy by taking care of your own physical and emotional needs first, loving yourself first. When you learn self-acceptance, compassion, and self-love, your fourth chakra expands and naturally and gracefully extends to others in a balanced way. Then your source of energy is limitless.

Achieving a state of balanced loving energy requires that you honor the subtlety of your feelings on all levels. What the feelings are is not as important as your ability to accept, recognize, and comfort the part of you that has that feeling. Again, it is not about changing the feeling — it is about being fully present with the feeling. Identifying your feelings and becoming a friendly observer of those feelings allows you to bring a charged subject into a more balanced and manageable form. It is about approaching yourself and life in a loving manner. In doing so, you reconnect with yourself on a deeper level, building trust and faith each step of the way. When you find yourself immersed in judgment, rejection, pain, grief, and other emotions that cause you to contract, bring kindness to yourself and others. Learn to see the humanity in all people. Allow a loving attitude to be present.

As the heart begins to open, the control of the ego diminishes. Life changes. What once drove the individual disappears. Often a time of deep transition follows. What once was truth is no longer. What was once identified as life no longer exists. One clearly sees the actions and events that one has created in the past that has kept love away. One clearly sees how separated and disconnected they are with their own spirit and with others. Often the opening of the heart can bring moments of deep grieving. This is the letting go of what was, so that the true authentic nature of the being can emerge. To grieve is to let the pain of past regret and losses move through the body. To grieve is to let the emotions of the soul emerge and express. A person grieves when they lose a loved one and a person grieves as they see how they have lost themselves. To let the emotions of grief emerge, is to continue to open the heart and release one's feelings. Grieving changes in every moment like all emotions, it takes a different form, shape and texture each time it arises and is expressed. Eventually the grieving turns to surrender, a deep sense of emptiness and connection held within the heart simultaneously. Then a new truth and experience emerges. If grief is not expressed the energy of the heart is blocked and contracted, creating isolation and aloneness.

"The heart center is the seat of a vaster, deeper kind of compassion and love-wisdom. It's about lovingness rather than just love. It is here that we can begin to glimpse the true nature of the soul and where we can feel our connection to everyone and everything."

Belleruth Naparstek,
Your Sixth Sense

Finding and feeling the heart energy can be both a painful and joyful experience. As the barriers of the heart are dispersed, tears of joy may arise. Joy often can be a newfound delight and feeling if one has been contracted in the heart. Joy stretches the walls of the heart begging for expansion. All encompassing joy fills the heart that has been emptied, the heart that has felt great pain, and the heart that longs for connection. The path to love is not always paved in roses, yet if one looks closely, one can see the roses are within arm's reach, waiting to be picked and shared with others. To live with joy is to reach for joy and to bring it into the whole being.

Balancing your feeling body and your physical body with your spiritual body is a key aspect in the heart chakra. We are feeling beings. We desire connection and love, with our own spirit and with others. To find the deeper levels of connection, we must be willing to open the door to our shadows and release the ego. One must be willing to let the feelings of life move through the heart, seeing both pain and pleasure as a part of the human experience. To live a life based and grounded in heart energy, one must be willing to love one's self, completely and unconditionally. It is then, and only then, that you experience the balance and depth of unconditional love and kindness toward others. This pathway leads to a life based on kindness, connection, love and joy.

Kindness in words creates confidence. Kindness in thinking creates profoundness. Kindness in giving creates love.

Lao-Tzu

fourth chakra details

Element:	Air
Sanskrit:	Anahata, un-struck, pure, un-broken
Color:	Green
Location:	Heart
Corresponding areas:	Chest, lower lungs, circulatory system, thymus, ribcage, arms
Theme:	Relationships/love
Core Shift:	I am in love. I love myself and others
Challenge:	Release grief and surrender to life

Balanced Characteristics:

Empathic, peaceful, openhearted individual that demonstrates a high level of self-acceptance as well as acceptance and compassion for others.

Signs of Imbalance:

Too much/Expanded	*Too little/Contracted*
Co-dependency	Shy, lonely
Poor boundaries	Isolated
Impatient	Depressed
Guise of super mature	Very immature
Jealous	Lacks compassion
Possessive	Bitter
Impatient	Critical, judgmental
Speedy	Dissatisfied
Looks to others for love	Low sense of self-love
	Feels hopeless

Physical Symptoms:

High blood pressure	Heart, lung, breast, thymus problems
Sunken chest	Circulation problems
Cancer	Heart Disease
Asthma	Chest pains
Tension between the shoulder blades	Shortness of breath
Shallow breathing	Skin disorders
Immune system disorders	

Signs of Balance:

∾ Perceived as a whole and loving person

∾ High level of appreciation of self and others

∾ Has accepted all aspects of self (shadow work)

  Is honest about feelings and thoughts

  Is content with life

  Lives a moderate and balanced life

  Has a sense of purpose and how to be of service

  Connects with others easily and gracefully with the heart

  Has strong, supportive, growth-oriented relationships with self and others

  Feels deep connection with self and others

  Is willing to take into the heart and body all experiences of life (joyful and painful)

  Receives and gives love easily

  Allows life to unfold without judgment

Goal:

  Achieve healthy, loving, nurturing relationships with self and others

Activities to Explore:

  Define what a balanced life would look like. Develop a plan of action to achieve this balance

  Explore the meaning of compassion. Establish three new action steps that will help you be more compassionate

  Explore the meaning of love and unconditional love, for yourself and others

  Develop daily actions of extreme self-love

  Fully accept who you are and who you are not

  Develop good strong relationships based on honesty and love

  Be content with your life

  Keep a journal listing what you appreciate about yourself

  Live with moderation in your relationships, your actions and what you consume

  Journal on topics such as love, forgiveness, compassion, self-love, and balance

  Write letters of forgiveness to self and others

  Send notes and cards expressing love and gratitude for others and yourself

  Maintain a daily "attitude of gratitude" journal

- ❧ Align your life work to be of service. Ask yourself "How may I serve?"

- ❧ Participate in exercises to strengthen and tone the heart: yoga, cross-country skiing, walking, rowing and biking

- ❧ Participate in exercises to stimulate and strengthen the lungs and heart: hang gliding, rappelling, ice-skating, ballet, parachuting, singing, and bicycle riding

- ❧ Bodywork: polarity therapy, massage (Swedish), meditation, breath work, yoga

- ❧ Release feelings and emotions of grief

- ❧ Increase your unconditional loving daily actions (and learn to receive these also!): hugs, touch another, give a gift, help a stranger, smile at a stranger, open a door for someone, let someone ahead of you in traffic

shifts for the fourth chakra

From...	To...
"I often judge others for their actions."	"I accept others in their weaknesses and strengths."
"There are many things I dislike about myself."	"I love and accept all sides, light and dark, of myself."
"My needs and agendas are most important and my first priority."	"I put people first at all times, objectives come second."
"I often feel shy and lonely."	"I feel a heart-felt connection with others."
"I often feel jealous and impatient."	"I feel comfortable and accepting of my interactions and relationships with others."
"Love evades me."	"Love is within me and all around me."
"He/she deserves what he/she gets."	"He/she was doing the best that he/she could."
"I don't like sharing my friends with others."	"The more, the merrier."
"Me, me, me."	"We, we, we."
"They could have done better."	"The situation is what it is, everyone is doing the best they can."
"I can do everything myself."	"Nothing in this world is worth doing alone, I want others to engage and help."
"I see what I don't like in others."	"I look for the beauty and gem in others."
"Everyone has love but me; I want to feel love."	"Love is within me, I must first cultivate love for myself so that I may unconditionally love others."
"I am most concern about how I fit into the picture with others."	"My life is based on how I connect with and can serve others."
"I want it now."	"I am patient and present to the flow of life."

Questions for journal work:
- What things do you do that demonstrate self-care and self-love?
- When do you feel compassion for others? When do you feel it for yourself?
- How might your life shift if you learned more compassion for others and yourself?
- What does 'unconditional love' mean to you? When and how does it show up in your life?
- What do you have a hard time accepting about yourself?
- How might things shift or change if you accepted these things about yourself?
- What do you feel when you hug someone?
- What is the quality of your breath?
- How might you increase your ability to listen to and feel your heart?
- What do you judge others about? Are you unhappy or out of integrity with yourself in these areas?

~ What gives you joy?

~ What can you focus on daily that will bring loving energy into your being?

~ What makes your heart sing?

~ What do you love about your family members, friends and colleagues?

~ When do you feel most connected to others? What are your thoughts, feelings and actions at those times?

~ What painful experiences of your life have you not released and grieved? How might your life and your energy level shift if you allowed yourself the time to process this painful experience?

~ Who would you have to be to have loving relationships with others?

Keywords:

Circulation	Love	Expansion
Air	Balance	Relationship
Compassion	Self-love	Peace
Contraction		

engaging the air and heart energy

In the second chakra, you explored your ability to feel. You explored pleasure, flow and emotions. What you do with your feelings and the choices you make in relationship to your feelings is an aspect of the heart chakra. It is not to say that you do not feel in your heart. In fact, if you are truly engaged with the energy of the heart you feel a lot! In the heart chakra, you take what you learned about sensing and feeling your emotions and you decide how you want to live your life, feelings and all.

For many people, an open heart means to give freely to others. To truly have an open heart means that you receive and take in the experiences of life, to truly feel what life is presenting you, whether you perceive the experiences as bad or good, and continue to flow and balance your life. An open heart is not a one-way street. It is a give and take, a flow back and forth, and a spiritual challenge for anyone on their spiritual path. Painful life experiences are inevitable. How you choose to take these experiences in and move through life is the skill and awareness to develop.

The energy of the heart chakra is the glue that holds the world together. It is the energy of how you connect and how you understand others, as individuals, and as a whole. To come from a place of heart-centered energy you shift from an "I" oriented position to a "we" or "us" oriented position. Heart-centered individuals value all life and all experiences as a part of the spiritual path. Nothing is separate. We are all part of a greater whole.

Heart Meditation

Using an upright chair, find a quiet place to sit. Sit with your back straight, tighten your buttocks and push your feet slightly into the ground, making firm contact. While keeping your buttocks tightened, lengthen your spinal column as if you are a puppet with a string at the top of your head. You remain seated. Allow your hands to float down by the sides of the chair, hanging freely. Slowly turn the palms of your hands outward pushing your chest forward and upward, stretching the front of your chest cavity. You may also engage your head by letting it slowly stretch back, as you look up toward the ceiling. Keep your buttocks tight and your legs grounded to support your lower back. Be gentle and kind as you feel the stretch in your chest and neck and slight arch in your back. Imagine there is a string attached to your chest, lifting it ever so gently.

Next, raise your head and bring it forward, letting your shoulders follow as your back comes to a straight position, releasing the arch. Your arms move forward and your palms now are facing inward toward your body. Round your back forward, vertebrae by vertebrae, and let your head hang loosely.

As you slowly breathe in, slowly roll your back and head upward again, arms and palms moving outward, buttocks still tight, shoulders and spine lifting, chest moving outward and the head stretching back, forming an arch in the back. Continue moving your body back and forth, arching and folding, in this way four to seven times. Breathe evenly and slowly, letting all of the air out of your body and bringing a full breath of new air into your body with each breathe. Breathe in on the upward flow and out as you fold down and inward. You may want to sigh as you release each breath. Notice where you might be tight or resisting the movement. Move gently and slowly, and do not push yourself. When you have finished, bring your awareness into your body. What are you noticing?

Place your hands on your legs; your palms toward the ceiling. Imagine a person or a pet that you love deeply. Bring a picture of them into your mind's eye. Let the warm feelings you have for them flood into your body and heart. Let a smile come across your face as you look at them admiringly in your mind's eye. Continue to breathe evenly as you enjoy the essence of their being and the love you feel in your heart for them. As you embody the love you feel for them, let the loving feeling grow and grow within you. Let the warmth fill your heart and warm your whole being. Sit. Fully engage with this energy.

With your palms facing up, on each hand bring your first finger and thumb together, forming a circular shape. Establish an intention that within the circles you have formed, you are capturing and connecting with the universal loving energy as you feel it in your body and heart at this time. Continue to sit for a few more minutes, bringing your awareness into your breath, feeling the energy of the heart and love.

Now in your mind's eye, imagine an image of yourself. Maintain the loving energy you felt previously. Direct this energy to this image of yourself. Let the warm loving feelings sink into your being. Let your hands help you to set an intention of keeping the loving heart energy moving through your body, spirit and heart. If any judgments or resistances arise, let them flow away with your breath. Breathe in love and breathe out love. Breathe evenly as you engage this energy for two to three minutes.

Next in your mind's eye place an image of someone you have difficulties with or struggle to understand. See this person as a person just as yourself, being human and living life. Bringing forth the same loving energy you have embodied previously, send this loving energy to the person in your mind's eye. Let yourself connect to the compassion you have for yourself and for them in this difficult time. Breathe loving energy into your heart and being as you see this person in your mind's eye. Say to yourself, "We are all one, as I see and feel you I see and feel myself, I release my anger/frustration/hurt/sadness and I release this energetic bond with love." Breathe deeply in and out as you feel love in your heart for the person in your mind's eye and for yourself.

Return once again to the first image you used of the person or pet you love dearly. Breathe in and out this loving energy restoring your heart and your whole body with love. Take several breaths, wiggle your toes, open your eyes, and congratulate yourself for working out your heart energy and muscle. Continue this exercise often. Like any workout program it becomes easier as you do it and the loving energy you experience will increase each time.

my fourth chakra summary

1. The insights I have about my fourth chakra are...

2. What I would like to focus on with regard to the fourth chakra is...

3. The three things I am willing to do to bring this chakra into balance and vitality are...

    1.

    2.

    3.

4. The behaviors and patterns I am willing to process, explore, release or give up are...

5. I am grateful for...

Fifth Chakra
Vishuddha

the fifth chakra assessment

Assess the vitality of this aspect of your life energy system. Place an "X" under the number that best represents the current status of each statement for you. Five is the highest ranking of level of truth. One represents the lowest level.

	1	2	3	4	5
People listen to me when I share my point of view and I feel heard.					
I am comfortable with silence and do not speak or chat to fill in the quiet space.					
I find it easy to articulate my thoughts when I speak to others.					
I do not gossip.					
I have a vision for my life and I can share this openly with others.					
I seldom interrupt others when they are speaking.					
I am a good, if not great, listener.					
My throat, ears, voice and neck are all healthy.					
I am a person who hears and speaks the truth.					
I realize the power behind words. I do not tolerate verbal abuse or language that is damaging.					
I can speak my opinion and thoughts clearly and precisely to individuals in authority.					
I have great timing and rhythm with words and sentences.					
I have strength in my voice and I fully utilize it.					
It is easy for me to acknowledge others and myself for accomplishments.					
I easily distinguish the tones and rhythms of the things I hear.					
I have something to offer the world and I am actively living my purpose.					
I have something that I feel and speak passionately about.					
I am responsible for creating my world through my actions, intentions and spoken word.					
I am aware of how the power of language and words. I do not use the 'word' against my spirit.					
I do not talk over other people when they are talking.					

Total of all Columns [   ]

Guide for Results:

80 – 100: Your vital energy in this chakra center is excellent at this time. Review the chapter to maintain your healthy balance.

60 – 79: Your vital energy in this chakra center is good at this time. Take some actions to increase your possibilities and energy levels.

40 – 59: Are you experiencing difficulties in certain areas of your life? Focus on this chakra to begin to balance and re-energize yourself.

20 – 39: Your vital energy is zapped in this chakra. Take some action today!

0 – 19: Yikes! Get into action now. You may want to seek professional counsel.

fifth chakra assessment questions

1. Which statements caught you off-guard, made you slightly uncomfortable, raised an eyebrow or caught your attention?

2. How do you feel after doing this assessment?

3. What areas of the assessment do you feel confident about?

4. What aspects of the assessment raised an emotional reaction in you? If so, what was your response?

5. What areas do you see that you might want to put some attention on releasing, healing, fixing, or creating? Please list these with three steps to support your growth in each area.

the fifth chakra: vishuddha

The fifth chakra is called Vishuddha, meaning purification or pure. It is located at the throat and governs your ability to communicate and your ability to bring your creative desires into the world. With a balanced fifth chakra, you will dance gracefully with others articulating your thoughts, feelings, and passions clearly and powerfully. This ability requires that you fully know the truth of your being and your path. In sharing this truth, and bringing it to the world through your voice, you manifest and create. The themes of the fifth chakra are communication and creativity. Communication is about how you hear, how you speak, what resonates with you, your intentions, and how you listen to what your body and senses are telling you. As the limitations of the lower chakras are released and healed, a person becomes heart based, living a more authentic life. Thoughts and feelings are based on love and intentions are clear and pure. This movement toward pureness is powerful. It is from this place of truth and purity that the true essence of the soul emerges.

"The words that enlighten the soul are more precious than jewels."

Hazrat Inayat Khan

The color for the fifth chakra is blue and it is located at the throat. This is the area where the air from the lungs is mixed with one's thoughts and comes out into the world in words. The element of the fifth chakra is sound. Words are, essentially, sound and vibration. Vibration is created as the particles and cells move at a particular speed. The rate of these particles moving determines the rate of vibration. The rate of vibration creates the quality of the sound. Each sound has its own individual vibration and intensity as it generates a different speed or movement based on the particles in the cells of its environment. Your relationship to these vibrations is what leads you through your life. You will naturally be drawn to the vibrations with which you most resonate. The process is similar to selecting music to listen to. Not only do you choose music that sounds good, but also music that makes you feel good physically and emotionally. You choose the music that resonates with you on these levels.

Each chakra has its own quality, color and element that reflects its unique vibration. Of all the chakras the first chakra has the heaviest vibration. The element of the first chakra is earth. Earth is heavy dense matter. The particles of this matter move at a much slower rate than the particles of air. As you have moved through the first, second, third, and fourth chakras you have explored different qualities and elements. As you move from the first to the seventh chakra, each one has a faster and lighter quality to it. Thus, the energy of the upper chakras is less dense and involves the less tangible qualities of life. The combination of all the chakras' health and vitality reflects the vibration of the whole being. As you explore the upper chakras (the fifth, sixth and seventh), you must consider the subtleties of your feelings, sensations, insights, and intuition, as they are the less tangible, though equally as important, qualities and elements of these chakras. These subtleties create a part of your energetic being. The energy of the fifth chakra engages one in exploring these subtle sensations.

Have you ever walked into a party and felt the vibe of the group of people? You might feel like you are going to have a good time. The music feels fun and lively. There is excitement in the air from the mixing and mingling. You sense an upbeat atmosphere or vibration. You sense that people are engaged and happy. Another party might feel completely different. The air may feel thick. The atmosphere may feel more hushed and confined. People are talking with their voices lowered. The room feels heavy. No one has told you anything about either party beforehand. Instead, your assessment is derived from using all your senses. You simply read the vibration on an intuitive, knowing level. You got a sense of what was going on. This way of sensing, with your whole body - your eyes, ears, nose, and skin, through the feeling of vibration, engages the fifth chakra energy.

The intangible qualities of the fifth chakra are experienced not in what can be seen, but rather what can be sensed through sound and other vibrations in an environment. As one's awareness of energy increases, one learns how to communicate on a much deeper level, with life and with others.

You discovered with the fourth chakra that the energy of the heart is often reflected in the manner in which one breathes. In the fifth chakra, breath mixes with thoughts creating words, and the tone and rhythm of words. All words have a vibration. If you choose to create a powerful life, you must learn to use the words that reflect the level of vibration you choose to create. It is easy to become unconscious to the words one uses. Words are a part of the way in which you create your world. If you truly wish to create a powerful, dynamic, loving life, select the words that make you feel self-respect, honor, and love for yourself and for others. Own the words you use. Choose words that move you forward versus words that hold you in place, or make you a victim. Choose words that lead you forward and increase your sense of personal power and possibilities.

Identifying the feeling you experience behind the words you speak is a key aspect in deepening your ability to communicate well. Unrealized feelings carry a charge that can slightly shift the energy and quality of one's tone. These unspoken intentions surround words. Intentions give words their energetic quality and vibration. Intention gives energy direction. The intentions behind words are often more powerful than the words used. Language brings energy directly to the outer world in the form of sound. From that place, energy begins to take form into matter. To become more conscious of the quality of intentions is to begin the process of purifying one's energy. If you choose words that inspire and empower you, and your intentions are clear and heart-based, you begin to create a vibration that is pure and clear to those around you. You then begin to attract the situations and people in your life that move you forward. If your thoughts are unclear and lack purity, you will attract events and people that reflect this energy back to you. You will maintain a state of confusion or ill feelings. Intention is energy not yet manifested in tangible reality. Once released and directed, intentions are powerful conductors of this energy. Who you are really are the intentions (thought forms) you hold within your being - the energy of your thoughts that vibrate within you and reside within your tissue.

"There exists for all of us, initially, a state of precommunication in which our intentions play across the body of another, and vice versa."

Merleau-Ponty

To fully communicate with others means to come from truth. If you are not fully in the "truth" of your life, ready and willing to share it with others, you will fall short in your communications and your attempt in being fully authentic. Truth is about expressing what is right and real for you. The truth is what feels best for you and what you know in your heart to be best for you. The truth is based on a sense of being fully within your own being, fully in touch with your own feelings, needs and wants. The truth is not about making someone else wrong or proving a point. It comes from one's inner core and sense of self. As you heal and shift the lower chakras, you begin to more easily identify and express your truths.

For instance, if someone asks you to do something that you feel uncomfortable doing, yet you agree to do it, although the truth is you really do not want to, you have moved away from your truth. The result is you may become angry, frustrated, bitter or have regrets about the situation. If the truth does not surface and the emotions are not resolved or expressed, you are withholding an aspect about yourself, your truth. In doing this you lose your vitality. This can show up in any aspect of your life: work, career changes, dating, relationships, family, education, sports and so on. Being truthful with the smaller aspects and choices one makes in life gives you more strength to be truthful with the larger more complicated situations. Pay attention to the connection between what you are feeling, what you are choosing to do, and how you communicate your intentions. Observe how well these two aspects (feelings and communications) are aligned with your truth. Is what you are saying really the truth for you? Is there more truth that you are not sharing? Are you feeling frustrated, yet telling others that things are fine? Do you find yourself being lead down paths that are not really where you want to go? If you have difficulty connecting with your truth, finish this sentence, in any situation, over and over, until the truth emerges, "The truth of the matter is...." Eventually you will peel back the layers of what is real and what is truth for you in any situation. From the place of truth make a new decision, take a new action, or express yourself in a different way.

What you say creates what you experience and bring forth in your life. If you are having a difficult experience in your life, you might ask a friend to be present with you for support. This creates more intimacy with that person. If you need some "alone time" to sort through your thoughts and feelings, you may request that a friend or partner leave you alone for a while. This creates solitude. You create your life through the words you share. You might also ask someone to go away when the truth is that you really want caring and comfort. Once again, you have stepped away from truth. This creates a mixed message. Your energetic body and heart are asking for comfort and you are articulating the desire for solitude. Your actions and communications are not aligned with the truth. Your ego is in denial or defensive and your being is longing for connection. To be in your truth, you must be real and authentic. You must first admit to yourself what your whole being is communicating to you, what you are feeling, what your heart is telling you, and what you truly desire. Then you must be willing to communicate that to others. What is the truth for you? What are you feeling? What are you communicating, or not communicating?

Dancing with the energy of another person is also a key factor in your communications. A dance is when two people move together in synchronicity, creating momentum and flow. To dance well, one must be able to anticipate the movement of another while being fully present and aware of one's self. The body and the senses are open and ready, not knowing for sure where the next step may be. By engaging your ability to sense subtleties, you begin to communicate on a level that includes both intention and caring. You learn to dance with and accept what is truth for yourself and what is truth for others. Mutual respect and trust is present. You learn to keep your truth. You also learn when you must keep your truth and depart from communicating with certain others who are not supporting you in your truth. The key word in our communications is "truth." When you step into what is true for you, in all aspects of your life, you can then, verbally and non-verbally, hold the space for the possibilities of creating a life based on that truth.

"Such is the irresistible nature of truth that all it asks, and all it wants, is the liberty of appearing."

Thomas Paine

"You never find yourself until you face the truth."

Pearl Bailey

When you reach your truth about who you are and how you want to be in the world, often the "energetic hooks" about how to achieve it diminish. Energetic hooks can be described as events or thoughts you create that have the intention of attachment. This means you consciously or unconsciously may be trying to produce a particular outcome. This usually includes aspects of trying, coercing others, extending your energy, manipulation, convincing, proving, or forcing a sale. Remember the saying, "the truth will set you free." The truth sets you free when it is fully integrated into your being. You believe in your ability to live in your truth. You are no longer trying to get anything or trying to prove anything about yourself. You have become your truth, your essence and your authentic self. When you are not aligned with your truth, you are in struggle, neglect, avoidance, addiction, fear, judgment, and other people's expectations. When this happens, you have dropped back down into the struggle aspects of the lower chakras. As you step more and more into your truth you are truly free from all that is not your truth. You live in your whole being, fully present. You have entered into engaging your spirit.

"I am a passionate seeker of truth which is but another name for God."

Gandhi

The more one is present, the deeper one can sense and communicate with others. The subtleties of how we listen are equally important to how we speak. When you listen with an open heart that is free of agendas and fear and full of trust, you create a space for others to show up and to be heard. This creates a safe space and a foundation for a lasting relationship. You are creating an open and safe atmosphere for others to engage with you. You must be in tune to another person's vibration to fully be able to communicate with this person. You must be open to understanding their experience and sensing the energy around what they are sharing with you. To do this you must remain curious about who they are and how they are experiencing life. Sensing and feeling the energy of communications helps one to intuit what is not being said with words. Often, what is not said in words, but sensed through energy, is a truth the speaker has not yet discovered. Sensitivity in listening deepens levels of understanding and respect with another. Pathways open to discoveries and creative collaborations. To conquer the skill of being fully present, engage the energy of body, mind and spirit.

Listening is a bonding action that ultimately creates connection. When you feel heard, you feel like you have been seen on many different and subtle levels. Every person is different, so every conversation we have with someone is a new experience. Communication is not something that you get and you move on to the next thing. Instead, communicating is about a dance of curiosity and discovery. Assumptions and predictions move to the side. Openness and emptiness allows one to hear and connect in present time. Communication is something we become conscious of on a moment-to-moment basis. Dancing with another's being (vibration) creates a synergy in which both people can express their essence. At that time we have stepped away from being "I" centered to a co-creating space where both beings can play together.

Regardless of whether you are speaking or listening, the key aspects of communication and creating include language, intention, sensing vibrations, and remaining curious, thus establishing a true presence. Stand back and observe yourself in your communications and continue to grow by exploring your capabilities. Learn to dance and weave with others, honoring their truth (being) and loving your own truth and being at the same time. Increase your awareness around the subtleties of your intention and how that creates your energetic being. Pay attention to who shows up in your life and what they are reflecting back to you. Pay attention to the truth of your words.

As the layers of communication and truth are peeled back, you may become more truthful about who you are and what you want in your life. Often, in this process, people realize that they are living a life that is not in alignment with 'who' they truly are. Many people base their life choices on a sense of obligation to others, expectations from family, or societal influences. As you dig deep into looking at what is true for you, you may find a core part of your life that is not aligned with your authenticity. In this way you can see how your spirit, your essential self, has been buried in a life based on a lie, a life based not on what you wish to create, but a life based on what you thought others expected you to create. This realization can be profound and painful for many to discover. The gift is that you can create what you want at any time of your life. You must be willing to do the work and to make the changes to live the life that is based on the truth of your being. Only you can move yourself into your most authentic expression. The first step is in articulating the truth of who you are and what you want.

Intention behind words will repel or attract others to you. When your intentions and actions are true to your being (third chakra) and when you are coming from the heart (fourth chakra), free of judgment and full of love, your communications carry a clear and pure vibration. When these words are backed with a deep understanding of your emotional motives (second chakra) and a sense of trust and foundation (first chakra), you are communicating at an even more congruent level. The bottom line is that you must step into the power of turning yourself into a skillful communicator (fifth chakra) to create what you want in your life. You must be able to clearly articulate who you are, what you stand for, what you feel passionate about, and what you want to create. As you speak your truth, your energy begins to align and vibrate out into the world. This in itself will attract the people who resonate with you. They are relating to your vibration. Then you have the community to support you in your creative endeavors and your dreams will become a reality.

"Every moment of your life is infinitely creative and the universe is endlessly bountiful. Just put forth a clear enough request, and your heart's desire must come to you."

Shakti Gawain

fifth chakra details

Element:	Sound, vibration
Sanskrit:	Vishuddha, purification
Color:	Blue
Location:	Throat
Corresponding areas:	Neck, thyroid, ears, mouth, jaw
Theme:	Communication and creativity
Core Shift	I speak my passion and truth with clarity and grace
Challenge:	Move away from creating untruths and lies, to being radically truthful and authentic

Balanced Characteristics:

An individual who has clear and concise communication skills, who is moving toward the life they choose by attracting others and situations that resonate with their vision.

Signs of Imbalance:

Too much/Expanded	*Too little/Contracted*
Arrogant	Fear of speaking
Better than	Lacks rhythm
Shameless	Worthlessness
Tyrant	Less than
Excessive talking	Shamed
Poor listening skills	Doormat
Talks over others	Stutters
Over-extended	Voice is low or trails off
Loud	Tone of voice is often 'down'
Fears silence	
Tone of voice is often 'up'	

Physical Symptoms:

Sore throats	Neck aches
Thyroid problems	Hearing problems
Asthma	Toxicity
Constantly clearing the throat	Jaw problems (TMJ)

Signs of Balance:

- Perceived as an articulate, powerful and creative individual

- Has the ability to clearly communicate to others the truth of any situation

- Is able to be fully present and listen to others
- Takes in and hears the rhythm and the messages in life
- Knows clearly what one resonates with or doesn't resonate with
- Has the ability to clearly communicate passions and life purpose
- Creates life through sharing visions, making requests and engaging others

Goal:
- Full expression of self-knowledge, passion and creativity

Activities to Explore:
- Begin to articulate your greatest desires
- Shift from use of self-deprecating language to language and words that honor your soul, spirit and being
- Speak your truth unconditionally
- Listen to music that engages your full being, music that you resonate with
- Develop deep listening skills
- Explore Neuro-Linguistic Patterning (NLP)
- Record your own affirmations and then listen to them daily
- Develop explorative questioning skills
- Explore creative ways to "be" (flow, presence, emptiness, openness)
- Tune into your energetic vibration, the vibration of others, and the vibration of environments
- Dialogue with your inner child
- Increase your verbal skills through storytelling, poetry, public speaking, singing, tuning, chanting
- Physical activities: primal screaming, cheerleading at your favorite organized sports event, team sports
- Bodywork: massage, chiropractic, Rolfing, cranial sacral, polarity therapy, reiki

shifts for the fifth chakra

From...	To...
"I often stutter or hesitate in my speech."	"I speak clearly and articulately about my thoughts, opinions and passions."
"I talk a lot and sometimes talk over or interrupt others."	"I gracefully communicate with others, dancing between listening and speaking."
"I am unclear as to what I want and how to let people know about what I want."	"I feel passionate about my message and my will drives me to share it with others."
"I have no direction or idea of how to connect with what is purposeful for me."	"I listen to the messages and pay attention to the signs and directions that life presents."
"It is not always clear to me what my next step or direction is."	"I listen to my body's wisdom and my intuition directs me."
"I am above this."	"This is something that I do not wish to participate in."
"I think you should be doing X, Y, Z - isn't it obvious?"	"Tell me more about what you think about the situation."
"I have lots of uncompleted business or communications with others."	"I have fully communicated the things I feel I want to with others - I feel free."
"I have no idea how to ask for what I want or need."	"I ask for what I want or need, knowing that I may not always receive what I am asking for in the way I originally imagined."
"I feel compelled to fill empty space with my voice, talking about all kinds of things."	"I am comfortable sitting silently with another and with myself."
"I seldom can sense when what someone else says sounds "off" or does not feel right to me."	"I pick up on the subtle vibrations in communications and I take note of these observations."
"Language is language, I simply say what comes to mind when it does."	"I am more conscious of the words and language I use in my communications. Words are powerful creators of energy and intention."

Questions for journal work:

- What do you most like to spend your time doing?
- What is your dream in life?
- What is your best communication skill?
- What communication skills would you like to improve?
- How do you read or pick up vibrations?
- When do you, if ever, clear your throat?
- What is your best listening skill?
- What do you resonate with?
- What do you enjoy listening to?

    What truths do you not share?

    What are the lies about your life that you have not faced?

    What is the intention behind your words?

    What phrases and words do you most often use in your verbal communications? How do these serve you or help you to communicate? (Explore use of slang, powerless speech and limiting language.)

    When do you avoid speaking up? How might your life change if you shifted this behavior?

    When do you tend to speak too much or say things you wish you hadn't? What new behavior would help to shift this pattern?

Keywords:

Communication	Vibration	Articulate
Listening	Throat	Creativity
Rhythm	Resonance	Intention
Alignment	Sound	

engaging the purifying energy of the fifth chakra

The Sanskrit word for the fifth chakra is Vishuddha, which means purification. Because all matter is moving and vibrating, one of the pathways to purify the whole being is through the use of sound and vibration. By using the voice for toning and chanting, you activate a vibration in your physical being and in all of the cells of your body. The body returns to its essential nature and states of being in this process. This is also why it is so important to become very conscious of the words and language choices you use. The words you speak vibrate in all of the cells of the body. The music you listen to and the words you hear from others can affect your energy field and vibration. Make conscious choices about what vibrations (words, sounds, energy, and colors) you allow in your life.

The throat chakra is the primary center for purification and activation of vibration and sound. It is at the throat that the air turns into sound coming out of the mouth. By engaging with meditations that use toning, humming and chanting we begin to harmonize the vibration of the throat area and the whole body. The act of chanting, humming and toning brings one back to center.

A mantra is a verbalization of sacred sounds that is repeated over and over in meditation and chanting. The vibration of mantras affects the nervous system and shifts the rhythm of the whole body, bringing the mind and body into a meditative state of consciousness and opening gateways to healing and purification. The word Mantra comes from the word *man*, referring to the mind, and *tra* that implies protection and instrument. A mantra is used as an instrument to clean, clear and protect the mind (thus the body and spirit) from useless or harmful thought patterns and information that bombards one's daily life, such as television and radio. Mantras may be used in silent meditation or vocalized as part of a meditation.

Each of the seven chakras has its own mantra (seed sound):

First Chakra	Lam (Lahm)
Second Chakra	Vam (Vahm)
Third Chakra	Ram (Rahm)
Fourth Chakra	Yam (Yahm)
Fifth Chakra	Ham (Hahm)
Sixth Chakra	Om (Ahm)
Seventh	Silence

Many Western practitioners prefer to use vowel sounds for chakras:

First Chakra	O as in row
Second Chakra	Oo as in due
Third Chakra	Ah as in father
Fourth Chakra	Ay as in day
Fifth Chakra	Ee as in see
Sixth Chakra	Mmm,nnn
Seventh	Ngngngng as in sing

There are many ways to engage the throat for balancing and healing. The Basic Humming Exercise will help you to begin to observe and activate your vibration body through the fifth chakra. Using the mantras for chanting, or the vowels for toning, will help you to deepen the integration of the vibrations in your whole being.

Basic Humming Exercise
Humming involves letting your breath move from the body with vibration. Sit quietly and observe your breath. Observe the flow outward and inward. Notice the subtle vibrations as air passes through your throat.

As air releases from your lungs, allow a sound to emerge from the throat. It does not matter what it sounds like. Let yourself experience your own tone and quality of sound without judgment.

Continue to let sound and air pass from your lungs and your throat. What particular sound or quality is most comfortable and naturally flowing from you? Continue with this sound, letting it merge into the hum. Continue humming your natural sound.

Notice and observe what happens in your body as you engage with humming for an extended period of time. Continue to hum up to five minutes. At the end of the five minutes, sit quietly and observe your body as you continue to breathe.

What happens to your mouth when you hum? Where do you feel vibration? What do you feel in your body as you continue to hum? When does it become more difficult or the quality of the sound decreases? What happened in your body at the different stages of humming? What happened in your body and mind as you stopped humming and became present with your breath? Remember, judging does not serve, simply observe.

Toning
Toning is much like humming in that there is a basic vibration of the body that comes through the throat. If you use the vowels for humming and

toning you may find that you must move your tongue to different areas of the mouth to better achieve the vowel vibration.

Chanting

Chanting is to use a simple phrase or sound in a repetitive manner to aid in bringing the body and mind into full resonance. Chanting can be done alone or with a group of people. Group chanting can be extremely powerful as many people begin to resonate together with the quality of the sound amplifying and taking on a life and energy of its own. It is magical and powerful for all involved.

Chanting

Sit in a comfortable position, either in a chair or on the floor sitting on top of your calves, or cross-legged in a more traditional meditative position. Let your hands face up toward the ceiling. Keep your back straight.

You may choose to work with one of the seed sounds for your mantra, or you may choose to spend several minutes on each seed sound moving through all the chakras, each with its distinct mantra. Repeat the seed sound you have picked for your mantra repetitively for several minutes. Pick the speed that works best for you. Some like to repeat the mantra rapidly. Others may prefer a slower paced repetition of the mantra.

If you choose to move from one chakra sound to the next I suggest you pause for one minute between each seed sound. This will let the vibration completely sink into your system before you move to the next sound. Continue with your chanting of the mantras for at least 20 minutes for very good results. You may continue after 20 minutes for as long as you wish.

Through this process notice what happens in your body and mind as you use the seed words as your mantras. What do you feel with each mantra and where do you feel the vibrations? How do the different mantras produce a different experience within you?

Affirmations

Affirmations are much like mantras. They are strong statements said only in the positive that reflect a feeling or result you want to integrate into your being. Your spirit does not recognize the words "no longer, anymore, will not," etc. Affirmations must also be present tense to be effective. An affirmation such as, "I will be centered and grounded in my life," leads to the future, it says, "I will be." Powerfully claim what you want, in the NOW, by using the present tense, "I AM centered and grounded in my life."

As you explore each of your chakra centers, you may want to develop an affirmation to use as your mantra to help you shift and open the energy you want to embrace with that chakra. Pick an affirmation that is doable and that you believe you are able to achieve. Use something you feel you are ready and willing to integrate. If you feel a major energetic block or wall come up with the affirmation you have selected, may want to pick a stepping stone affirmation that will help work your way to the bigger and more powerful affirmation. This is a powerful way to tap into the energy that is you and to be the creator of your life. Be precise and careful with your affirmations. What you ask for you shall receive.

my fifth chakra summary

1. The insights I have about my fifth chakra are ...

2. What I would like to focus on with regard to the fifth chakra is...

3. The three things I am willing to do to bring this chakra into balance and vitality are...

    1.

    2.

    3.

4. The behaviors and patterns I am willing to process, explore, release or give up are...

5. I am grateful for...

Sixth Chakra

Ajna

the sixth chakra assessment

Assess the vitality of this aspect of your life energy system. Place an "X" under the number that best represents the current status of each statement for you. Five is the highest ranking of level of truth. One represents the lowest level.

	1	2	3	4	5
I have a strong relationship with my intuition and I listen to it.					
I can access and remember dreams.					
Visualization is an easy thing for me to do and experience.					
I clearly see what is going on in my life and my role in it.					
I am sensitive to those around me.					
It is not difficult for me to concentrate.					
There is nothing that I excessively obsess about.					
I do not have nightmares.					
I grew up in a non-violent environment.					
My memory is very good.					
I have a great imagination.					
I do not suffer from headaches.					
I do not suffer from vision problems.					
I tune into the things that occur in my life and pay attention to synchronistic happenings.					
I apply attention to my inner thoughts and fantasies and use them to deepen my understanding of myself.					
I have an optimistic point of view.					
I have explored the re-occurring patterns and themes in my life.					
I use my intuition to make daily decisions.					
I am living and sharing my vision.					
I have a positive outlook on life and people.					

Total of all Columns

Guide for Results:

80 – 100: Your vital energy in this chakra center is excellent at this time. Review the chapter to maintain your healthy balance.

60 – 79: Your vital energy in this chakra center is good at this time. Take some actions to increase your possibilities and energy levels.

40 – 59: Are you experiencing difficulties in certain areas of your life? Focus on this chakra to begin to balance and re-energize yourself.

20 – 39: Your vital energy is zapped in this chakra. Take some action today!

0 – 19: Yikes! Get into action now. You may want to seek professional counsel.

sixth chakra assessment questions

1. Which statements caught you off-guard, made you slightly uncomfortable, raised an eyebrow or caught your attention?

2. How do you feel after doing this assessment?

3. What areas of the assessment do you feel confident about?

4. What aspects of the assessment raised an emotional reaction in you? If so, what was your response?

5. What areas do you see that you might want to put some attention on releasing, healing, fixing, or creating? Please list these with three steps to support your growth in each area.

the sixth chakra: ajna

*T*he sixth chakra is called Ajna. It is located between the eyes and is often referred to as the third eye or the mind's eye. This chakra represents how you see and what you choose to see in the world. The color of this chakra is indigo; the element is light. Light provides us the opportunity to see and explore the brilliance, multitude of dimensions and depth of different situations in your life and in the world. Light shines in your life, regardless if your eyes are open or shut. Your dreams, intuition, and visions play a significant role with this chakra. People with a balanced sixth chakra can combine their logic, or what they see as real in the world, with what they see as possible or know to be the right direction due to felt senses, visions, and intuitive guidance. Those with a balanced sixth chakra are open to the images and insights that come to them randomly in life. They use these images and insights as part of the path, process, and connection to the universe that is guiding them. Engaging the sixth chakra energy allows one to also see the beauty of color, texture, tones and shapes of the world.

Light shines in your life to illuminate your path. Without light in your life, you can only make choices based on logic or what makes sense based on the processes of your mind. If your choices and decisions are based primarily on logic, you are not using all the resources available to you. You are functioning partly in the dark; you are not engaging the sixth chakra, the chakra of light. The rational mind may try very hard to make right decisions. But in your body, in your gut, or through an intangible knowing, the decision may not feel right. You might not really be able to see what is missing or what is not aligned properly, but you will sense it intuitively. By using this intuitive information, you can shape your life using all of the sensing tools available to you with the logical thinking part or your mind.

Without using the tool of the sixth chakra and the power of light, you are depending fully on your mind to carry you through any situation. The mind works well for you and must be an integral part of your life. Yet, you know that there is more to you than just your mind. You have discovered this in the first through fifth chakras. Using pure logic without the knowledge or information from your body limits your intuitive ability to create advantageous life strategies. To live powerfully, you must claim your relationship with all the resources available to you, such as your body. In the case of the sixth chakra, you must heighten your ability to connect with the light, your visions, your dreams, and your intuition as a resource and guiding force in your life. Embracing these aspects takes your knowledge base to an even greater level of integrity and wholeness.

When you begin to perceive and interpret on many different levels, your life takes on a more graceful and expedient path. You are allowing yourself to trust your instincts and the unexplainable visions you have with regard to your path, projects, challenges or even in your everyday existence. You live differently, beginning to live with the universal energy, asking for guidance and paying attention when it shows up.

What exactly is light? Light illuminates what we look at and gives an object depth and definition; it is a source of illumination. Sometimes people say, "I finally saw the light." They are referring to the fact that they understood something on a deeper, more profound level, or the missing link to a piece of the puzzle suddenly came into view. They may have been able to fit the pieces of a situation together in a more understandable way, or, maybe their thoughts came together differently, finally allowing them to make sense of a situation. It is as if the light was suddenly turned on. Just like the cartoon character with the light bulb over his head when he gets a brilliant insight or idea, intuitive insights happen in the same way. These insights can be sudden, and often come from "out of the blue." How appropriate that the sixth chakra color is indigo blue!

Intuition comes in many forms. Dreams may take on significant meaning in your life, serendipitous events may change your course or view of something, you may experience visions about how some event may turn out, and/or unexpected thoughts may randomly come to you at any given time. These events signify an active and engaged sixth chakra. As you work with the sixth chakra your life will begin to flow and move like magic. Often, these insights or moments of intuition may be so profound and startling that you might be tempted to shut the valve off, ignore the message, and no longer permit these images through your mind's eye.

Seeing into the possibilities of the future might frighten you, as you may have been raised to believe that such things are only our imagination, silly games that young people play, inappropriate behaviors, or the information can't be trusted or believed. Yet, intuition is merely seeing the possibilities of the future. Intuition is about sensing how energy may take form and manifest on the physical plane. It is not about what a person wants to have happen in the future. Instead, intuition enters the mind's eye at random times, offering

"Our eyes are, or course, our main sensory means for receiving light into our bodies and transforming the information carried by reflected light into visual images that give us our impressions of the outside world."

John Selby,
Kundalini Awakening

"Our sixth sense or clairvoyance (clear seeing) is developed in the third eye chakra where we attain an inner sense of knowing and live in the magic and possibilities of our life."

Jaya Sarada,
The Path of Return

random insights and messages. These messages are clear and direct and most often occur when there is knowledge and acceptance of what has been seen. It is your job as an adult to reconnect to this energy if you have lost it. In doing this you fully claim the power you possess to enter into a natural flow of life based on using all of your senses. In doing so, you reconnect to an authentic vision of your path and purpose in life.

Serendipitous events happen all the time. They can be small or substantial. You may think of how you might like to connect with a long-lost friend. You might be holding that vision in your mind's eye. Is it really a surprise to you when they call or contact you? You have been holding the vision for the connection without any doubt or reason to believe you will not connect with them. Energetically you have already created the arena for the event. The other person picks up on this energy and shows up in your life. Another time you might be thinking about taking a new training or workshop. Is it surprising that information about that workshop pops up in your world in strange and unexpected ways? These serendipitous events are actually signposts along your path to lead you in a direction you could choose to go. When I was writing this chapter I thought to myself that I wanted some examples of serendipitous events that demonstrate how one can be lead by the signs life presents. I wrote this chapter on a Friday. On Saturday, I went to a seminar in the city. On the way to lunch, I glanced at a shop across the street. The name of the shop was "The Third Eye." It is the only shop I have ever come across with this name. This serendipitous event confirmed for me that I was on the right track and that a wonderful example was right before my very eyes. Fortunately, my eyes were open to receiving this visual message.

"What I am actually saying is that we need to be willing to let our intuition guide us, and be willing to follow that guidance directly and fearlessly."

Shakti Gawain

We have a choice if we want to pay attention to these occurrences or not. I had a client who was going through a life and work transition. He told me that out of the blue he had a thought about being a real estate salesperson. That next weekend he saw an advertisement in the local paper advertising a real estate position that included training. Later that day he met up with an old friend. The friend told my client that he was currently a real estate appraiser and that he loved his work. My client did not act on these signs at the time. Two years later, he did take some actions and made some decisions that brought him into the real estate profession. The energy was available to him earlier. His next occupation was knocking on his life door. He chose to wait and he still created it later. The pieces of his life puzzle were showing up at different times, so, as he saw them, he fit them together.

We all know the stories of people who meet and know in that instant that they have met their life partners. They intuit this information and embrace it without doubt. To heighten your awareness of how the universe shines light on your life, begin to pay attention to what is showing up in your life regarding what you are thinking and talking about. How is what you see helping you to define your path and make decisions on both a smaller daily level and on a grander life-decision level?

Have you ever experienced having a vision flash, pass, or float through your mind that seems out of context for the setting you are in? Perhaps the vision is in the future or not appropriate to today's world. These flashes of light or insight are packed with information for you to use on your life path. What is happening is that you are picking up on the subtle vibrations of light that are available to you. Your mind's eye then interprets these vibrations and they appear as visions or pictures that flash before you. Life becomes magical when we pay attention to these visions and act with the knowledge or insights we derive from them.

The power of insights and intuition can often be a scary experience. In my late teens and early twenties, I often picked up on tragedies and accidents that were about to occur. Because of my lack of understanding of what was really happening I felt responsible for what had happened. I thought that on some level, because I had seen and sensed the imminent danger and disaster in my mind, that I should have said something to prevent it. Thus, I closed down this powerful source of connection with the universal energy. Now as an adult, I can put the context of my insights into a more understandable format and then make choices on how I want to take this information into the world. As you become more open to the intuitive visions you may begin to experience, you may also need to learn how to set an intention on when you want this channel to be open. To create the life you want you must have the sixth chakra open and working in a balanced way that will lead you more effortlessly along your path.

This is where your intuition lives, in your mind's eye. When the mind's eye is active, one is more open to receiving and perceiving the world around them. A healthy sixth chakra will support the opening and sensing of your whole being. You have learned with the lower chakras how you use your body to increase your wisdom of the energy of your environment, the people around you, and your own state of energy. This is your body wisdom. This wisdom blends with your intuition. A high level of body wisdom works hand in hand with your intuition. Gut feelings come from the body, yet those sensations are part of your intuition. When you get a funny feeling about something, your intuition is speaking through you. Does your increased perception of energy interpretation from using your body support your ability to be intuitive? YES! Increasing your ability to use your body as a source of information heightens your ability to communicate on many levels. You become more

"Opening the third eye allows us to see the big picture, transcend our egocentricity, and find the deeper meaning inherent in all things."

Anodea Judith,
Eastern Body Western
Mind

sensitive and open to energetic communications. Remember that you are generating energy in each of your chakras so that you can create the life you want, drawing from all the energy and resources available to you.

Your intuition may come in the form of visions. Some individuals experience intuitive messages in the form of voices or sounds, thoughts that flash through their head, and/ or images and visuals in the mind's eye. These are all signs of connecting with one's intuitive abilities. All people have intuitive abilities. Some people must practice and work at developing the skill. Work with these pieces and pay attention to them. Allow them to lead you and take you along your path. Sometimes, it is as simple as a voice in your mind that says, "Go to the window," or "Call your friend right now." When you listen to these messages and take action, you connect with the things and people who want to connect with you. Your ability to act on your intuition creates a life of synergy, gathering more serendipitous but significant meetings, chance encounters, or well-timed misses.

"Your intuition has a more refined understanding of your right life than any other part of consciousness."

Martha Beck,
Finding Your Own
North Star

Your ability to live a life supported by your intuition requires you sometimes to move your logic aside. For instance, the writing of this workbook is not based on a logical, well thought out business plan. Instead, I was drawn on an intuitive level to begin the process. What originally was going to be a basic twenty-page workbook has grown magically into a much richer workbook filled with useful information and material. When I applied to present at the International Coach Federation conference in 2001, I intuitively knew that I would be accepted. I had no idea what I would really be presenting, but I intuitively knew I had to send an application and that I would be speaking at the conference. Because I followed this intuition, I spoke at the conference, found several people interested in the topic of energy and chakras, launched a class, and have continued to develop this workbook. I can see clearly the light shining on my path. Though I may lack the knowledge of how all the pieces are going to come together, I know that it is the path I must take and that even more will come of it. It is as if a force much greater than me is providing me with even more energy to complete the task. So, even though logically it does not make the most sense, I stay on this path. You must trust your intuition, the pulls of your consciousness that say do this, look here, go there, wait, talk to this person, buy this book, call this person, look in this store, etc. even when it really does not make a lot of logical sense. Look to your life to see the recurring thoughts you have had about your life's path and begin to follow these signs and intuitive hits.

When your sixth chakra is open and balanced, you become more aware of and are able to see the patterns you create in your life. As the light shines on your life, you gain clarity. These may be patterns that support you in your growth or patterns that keep you from your growth. Understanding the complexity of patterns requires you to be able to be an observer of your actions and the events of your life. You must be able to consider not only the most recent events, but also those from the past. You must be able to see the actions and events that, with different people and at different times, have created the same results, experiences and feelings about yourself. This is the creation of patterns. You continue to have the same experience or feeling at different times in your life. Increasing your awareness of these patterns puts you back into the driver's seat of your life. You may have a great vision for your future; if you do not have the ability to see the patterns that your thoughts or actions create, you might be limited in your success.

From your childhood, you begin to formulate your experiences. You may think that parents behave a certain way, couples interact in a particular manner, men do one thing, women do another thing, and that if you do ABC you will get XYZ. Your experiences help you to make better decisions in your future. You get into trouble when your experiences have made a concrete belief pattern that keeps you in the same experience over and over. From the observations you made as a child, you drew conclusions. These conclusions later developed into a belief system and this belief system has ultimately limited your ability to create as an adult. In the sixth chakra, you see the beliefs that run the energy in all of the other chakras. Beliefs are the cornerstone of how you create your life. How you see your life is based on what you believe to be true in what you see. You take in your experiences and perceptions and form your beliefs. Your thoughts, emotions and actions are all based on these initial perceptions and beliefs.

Often, seeing your patterns will lead you to the undoing of your perceptions about how things happen in life. When you engage in and explore these patterns, you gain control over who you are and how you create. Patterns can often serve you or limit you. Allowing repetitive thought patterns will bring the same results, thus confirming the original belief and pattern. The key is to identify the patterns that show up in your life and shift these patterns for different results. Working with the insights that the energy of the sixth chakra provides is the beginning. Notice the dissatisfying areas in your life and explore the themes that occur there. You may find the pattern or programming is based in one of the lower chakras, but that your ability to see the patterns emerges as you gain more openness in the sixth chakra. Also, explore the positive patterns that have led you to success and replicate these patterns in the areas you want to change.

How well do you observe what is unfolding in your life around you? How well do you sense the dynamics of any event? How do you perceive how

"In the recognition of patterns, we find our way to insight. Insight is the ability to see within, the "aha" of recognizing a pattern, seeing where it relates to the larger picture, seeing what it means."

Anodea Judith, Eastern Body Western Mind

"Seeing ourselves as we really are is one of the most difficult things we are called to do."

Johanna Putnoi, Senses Wide Open

people interact with other people? It is the ability to sense the outcome and unfolding of things, before they actually happen, that gives us power in our own life and also as leaders for others. Heightening your ability to perceive and intuit puts you in a position to make small shifts that can dynamically alter the outcome to be more fortuitous for all involved. Good leaders are able to do this. Good leaders are always in tune with the possibilities that are unfolding and know how to focus themselves or the group to achieve the most positive result from the possibilities that are available. They can intuit the synergy of a group and use that intuitive knowledge to lead gracefully and successfully.

"If you believe that your dreams are impossible, then they will be. The movers and the shakers who grab an idea and run with it believe in their vision."

Lucia Capacchione, Ph.D., Visioning

You might become stuck in your life and not be able to make a decision based on logic or draw any sort of intuitive information. Exploring the use of dreams is another way to expand the sixth chakra energy. Dreams are another dimension in which we live. Dreams are another reality that many of us experience and often do not fully explore. Setting an intention to receive clarity around a challenge or situation you are struggling with during your dreaming time can be a profound tool and opening for your daily life. Set an intention for clarity around an area you feel you need light in. Also, set the intention that you will remember the insight. Keep a pad of paper next to your bed. If you wake up in the middle of the night journal your dreams. In the morning, when you wake up, journal what you remember. Use this process to explore your imagination and the world of your subconscious. You will find many helpful insights in this process.

As you increase your ability to let the serendipitous events of your life lead you down your path, your intuition will naturally increase. You will also begin to formulate a clear vision of what it is you want to create in your life. You will see pieces of your life purpose come to your mind's eye. Capture these visions through journal activities, drawing and other means of visual expression. One of the most powerful ways to manifest is to build a collage of what your vision is. After creating a collage of pictures that capture the essence of what you want to create, you can meditate and focus on this visual to pull the energy of this vision into your mind and into your whole being. You are bringing the energy of the vision closer to your life. You are setting the energetic stage that will ultimately attract and welcome your vision. It can be a powerful and profound process.

If you cannot see your vision, most likely you will not create it. If you cannot perceive it really happening, if you cannot believe in the possibility, it will never happen. Things happen to people who believe things can happen. They carry a torch to light their way. They are unbending in their vision and the belief of the vision coming to life. When your vision is clear and congruent with your being, the alignment of the energy draws your vision to you. Yet, you must also remain unattached to how the vision shows up in your life. This means that how we might visually dream it might not be exactly how it might look when it arrives. However, it will arrive with the same essence or energy. The first step is to let yourself dream it and see it.

How you perceive yourself and how you think others perceive you will determine how you create your life. If you perceive yourself as a strong, capable person with a lot of potential, you mostly likely will be able to move forward with life changes and challenges. If you perceive yourself as someone who has little or nothing to offer others, you will mostly likely continue to experience situations that perpetuate more of the same experience. That is the energy you are putting out into the world and that is the energy you hold for yourself. Even if a person sees your potential and offers you a situation in which you can contribute, you will have difficulty experiencing that for yourself. If you cannot see that you have something to contribute, you will not be able to fully integrate the feeling of contributing into your being. Your perception of yourself keeps you creating the same perception over and over, until awareness is brought to the limiting perception you have. Looking at how you perceive yourself, in your life and in your interactions with others, will help you to remove perceptions that do not move you forward and are not the truth about who you really are. Once these limiting perceptions are lifted, you are back in the flow of your life.

"The picturing power of the mind is now being rediscovered by psychologists, who say that imagination is one of our strongest mind powers."

Catherine Ponder, Open Your Mind to Prosperity

Serendipitous events and intuitive insights are not to be noticed with awe and excitement. Instead, these events are to be held with expectancy as a sign that you and the universe are working together in your everyday existence and in the bigger picture of creation of your passions and life. Defining such events as special, unique or mysterious separates these events from you. You then position yourself as someone life 'happens to' versus someone who is in union with the universal energy. Live your life with expectancy and you are living WITH the universal energy or source that is constantly available to you and all life on the earth.

Open yourself to your insights; ask for guidance from an intelligence that exists beyond that which we understand. Balance your logical thinking with that which shows up in front of you that guides and leads you in ways that sometimes seem contrary to what you really want. Notice the patterns you create and make conscious decisions about how you may want to shift these perceptions. Embrace the pleasure of enjoying your dreams and visions and the possibilities that lie in bringing them to light. Remain consistently true to your vision and ultimately unattached to how or when the pieces come together. Dare to dream, dare to see and dare to believe you can create your vision.

"The future belongs to those who believe in the beauty of their dreams."

Eleanor Roosevelt

sixth chakra details

Element:	Light
Sanskrit:	Ajna, servant, to command
Color:	Indigo
Location:	Forehead, between eyes
Corresponding areas:	Eyes, ears, nose, nervous system, pineal gland
Theme:	Intuition, life patterns
Core Shift:	I see the vision of my life's path
Challenge:	Shift any illusions you have and accept the truth of the present reality

Balanced Characteristics:

An individual who demonstrates a high level of intuition and vision.

Signs of Imbalance:

Too much/Expanded	*Too little/Contracted*
Headaches	Poor memory
Nightmares	Poor vision
Hallucinations	Can't see patterns in life
Constantly has new ideas	Has no vision of life path
Delusions	Denial
Difficulty concentrating	Insensitive
Excessive use of intuition	Can't remember dreams

Physical Symptoms:

Headaches	Glaucoma
Injuries to the head	Poor vision
Infections/problems of the eyes	Nightmares

Signs of Balance:

- ↜ Insightful person
- ↜ Use of intuitive skills as part of life decisions and process
- ↜ Exploration of symbolic meaning and incorporation of this into life
- ↜ Able to recall and remember important dates, names, etc. when needed
- ↜ Life work is accomplished by the sense of spirit working through the individual
- ↜ Use of patterns found in nature and human behavior is applied for life development
- ↜ Uses imagination skillfully

Goal:

∾ Increase your ability to use your intuition and inner wisdom in making choices and decisions

Activities to Explore:

∾ Activities to increase your memory muscles

∾ Recognize the patterns in your everyday life and work life

∾ Record your dreams in a journal. Explore and seek clarity about the symbols and events in your dreams through additional journaling

∾ Visual stimulation (the arts, nature, etc.)

∾ Participation in visual art activities

∾ Recognition of serendipitous events or thoughts

∾ Taking actions when you get an intuitive thought, sense or message

∾ Collages, vision boards, mandala artwork, or drawing

∾ Meditation

∾ Hypnotherapy

shifts for the sixth chakra

From...	To...
"I just can't see what is right for me or where I should go next."	"I clearly see my purpose and my position and events in my life."
"I don't see the connections in the events of my life."	"I see the patterns in my life and how these patterns affect my ability to manifest."
"My memory is bad and I often have headaches."	"I have clarity of eyesight and also my mind feels clear."
"I can't find the right answer and many times I feel confused."	"I have enough time, space and inner silence that I can hear guidance when it emerges."
"This is not what I had envisioned."	"I clearly see what is showing up in my life."
"The same things keeps happening to me and I do not understand why."	"I see how the things I think, do and say create the same patterns in my life."
"I can not sense what is the right direction for me."	"I am developing a strong sense of trust and knowing. This leads me to easier life choices."
"I get a vision, a gut feeling or intuitive thought and then my mind questions and I lose my strength in deciding what is best."	"I let my intuitive knowing easily blend with my logic and analytical thinking so I can make powerful life choices."

Questions for journal work:

- Describe in full detail one of the fondest memories in your life (what did you hear, feel, think, taste, smell, etc.).
- What are the recurring patterns that you see in your life?
- How do these patterns serve you? Or not serve you?
- What new patterns would you like to embrace in your life?
- How does your intuition emerge in your life?
- When do you feel most intuitive?
- What is the image that you have of yourself? What do you identify with?
- How important is your image? What do you sacrifice to uphold this image?
- What type of serendipitous events have you experienced in your life?
- What messages or images seem to pop into your life over and over?
- What did you dream last night?

Keywords:

Light	Darkness	Vision
Patterns	Dreams	Memory
Visualization		

meditation to engage the energy of the third eye

This meditation serves a dual purpose. The first aspect of the meditation will help you to clear your whole energy system of toxic energy or energy that is simply no longer serving you. Once that energy is cleared from your system, the second aspect of the meditation will help you to engage the energy of your 'Third Eye' or the sixth chakra. As you engage the sixth chakra energy, you will increase your ability to intuit the energy of each of your seven chakras through seeing colors, shapes, patterns and textures within each center. There is no right or wrong way to do this meditation. The most important aspect is to become aware of what you are sensing, remaining open and trusting yourself in the process.

Prepare a space where you can have quiet time, uninterrupted by a phone or other people. Sit in a comfortable chair, feet on the floor, hands on legs, palms facing the ceiling with your eyes closed. Take a few breaths and bring your awareness into your body.

Starting from the head down to your feet begin to sense your energetic self. Notice the quality of energy all around and in your body. Notice where you sense more energy and where you have a more difficult time connecting with your energetic self (observe yourself only, self-judgment is unacceptable and contradictory to the purpose of meditation). Notice the quality of the energy you are sensing. What is the color of your energy? What is the density? Do you sense movement, thickness, heat, coolness or tingling around you? Does it move or flow and, if so, how fast? Can you feel energy all around and in your body? Set your intention to connect with the areas that are harder to sense. Be patient and continue to observe as you set this intention.

After you have a good sense of your energetic being, bring your awareness to the ground below you and the earth energy. Bring all your attention to the grounding quality of the earth energy. Imagine this energy running up into your feet, legs and pelvic area and all the way up through your head. You might feel a heaviness, see brownish-red colors or have a sense of being more still and contained in your body. Observe as this energy rises in your body. What do you experience in your body? Is your heart rate slowing down or speeding up? How is your breath changing? What sensations are present in your pelvic area, your torso and your upper chest area?

Once you are fully connected to grounded energy, set your intention to attach any negative energy, or energy that is not yours or that is no longer useful for you, that is in your system, to the grounding energy you have brought into your body. Let all of this energy connect to the grounding energy. Now, imagine this energy flowing back out of your body, down through your limbs and out your feet. Flush this reddish-brown energy out your feet sending it down to the center of the earth, taking with it all the toxins and negativity you want to release. Empty your whole body and energy field of this grounding energy.

Now, bring your attention to the seventh chakra. Let the energy of the universe come into your head and down through your body. Let this energy pour through your whole being. Imagine this light and bright energy seeping into all of your body. Sense how your energy has shifted. What do you feel at this time? What do you sense?

Once you have experienced the energy from the universe running through your whole body, bring awareness to your feet. Once again, imagine the grounding energy moving back into and through your feet, your legs and into your stomach or solar plexus area. Mix the energy of the earth and the energy of the universe together, in your third or fourth chakra, where it feels most comfortable to you. Imagine this energy swirling together, balancing and centering your whole energy being. Feel yourself fully centered, grounded and open to the energy of the universe.

Begin now to focus on your first chakra. Observe any sensations you have in this area, letting yourself wander and observe, without making any judgments or drawing any conclusions. As you sense and observe, let your third eye begin to also observe and intuit what it might see in this area. You may have a sense of a color or a gradation of tone. You may see images or pictures, you may see a disk-like shape, or you may see patterns. Let you mind's eye observe and intuit what lies in your first chakra. What is it that you see there?

After you have fully observed the textures, shapes and colors of your first chakra, you will begin to release any negative energy or ties to others that are no longer serving you. At this time ask yourself, "Self, what energy am I ready to release?" As you ask the question, pay attention to the images, faces, colors or shapes that might enter your mind's eye. Without questioning what you see or sense, gently imagine this energy and imagine leaving your energy field and returning to the ethers or to the person in your mind's eye. As you do so, you may see strings, cords, or rope-like images that are connecting you to this other person. Gently and slowly allow these strings to detach from your energy center. Let your mind's eye show you the energy leaving your chakra. Continue to release energy, until you feel you have cleared your chakra of negative energy that is no longer serving you. Take notice as to what you perceive in your sixth chakra at this time.

When you have completed the first chakra, move upward through each chakra, sensing, observing, and releasing energy. Continue to focus on allowing your mind's eye to be open and active in this process. Allow the visuals to come through your mind's eye without judgment.

As you reach and complete the seventh chakra, imagine a bright sun surrounding your head. It is larger than life and your head rests gently within this brilliant sun. The sun represents your authentic energy. Set an intention to bring the energy from the sun into your body. Imagine your brilliant energy filling all of your cells. Feel the lightness and warmth as you connect with all of your life force and essential self. Fill yourself with all which you are. Sit with this wonderful vibration for at least 20 seconds.

Now, bring your awareness back down to the grounding energy once again. Remind yourself of the wonderful connection you have with the earth energy. Feel fully grounded to the earth and present in your whole body.

Open your eyes. Bend at the waist, hang your head and shake your arms and hands. Wiggle your toes, open your eyes and bring your awareness to your environment. Notice the quality of your seeing and sensing at this time.

Continue to work with this meditation. Actively engage the power of your mind's eye to sense and see the images, textures, shapes, and colors that might appear in each chakra. You need not be concerned if the color you see in a chakra is not the color that represents that chakra. Energy is constantly moving and every individual expresses energy differently. Let yourself be free of any judgments or constraints. Do not try to implant a color into your chakra. Instead, allow your mind's eye to see what is there to begin with. Enjoy the unfolding of the visuals.

As you grow more confident at directing the power of your mind's eye to interpret the energy of each of your chakras you may eventually shift to bringing in different colors to fill the space that you have cleared. It is important to first learn how to observe and see what is within your energy, before you begin to intentionally direct with visuals such as color. This meditation is designed to open your ability to intuit and see what lies in each of your chakra centers. Each time you do this you will see and sense different things.

Continue to work with your mind's eye everyday in this way. Eventually you may find that your sense of intuition in general begins to increase as your energy becomes clearer and clearer, free of the negativity that you may have picked up in environments and from other people. As you continue to create the space for your mind's eye to explore and express, you are honing your muscle of intuition. In your everyday life you may start to get a sense or see images that direct you and guide you in your decision making processes. You may feel as though you have a stronger sense of perception and a broader scope of seeing in general.

You must consciously practice to be free of judgments or criticism in this process. Be gentle with your thoughts, be kind in the process of releasing, and embrace the learning that you experience with gratitude.

my sixth chakra summary

1. The insights I have about my sixth chakra are ...

2. What I would like to focus on with regard to the sixth chakra is...

3. The three things I am willing to do to bring this chakra into balance and vitality are...

    1.

    2.

    3.

4. The behaviors and patterns I am willing to process, explore, release or give up are...

5. I am grateful for...

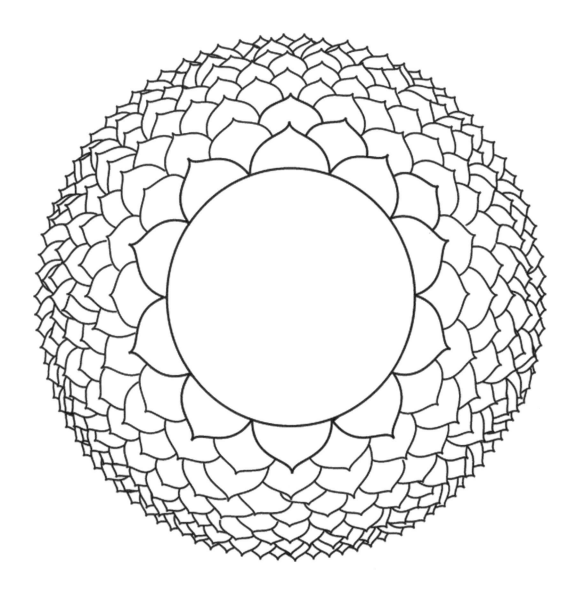

Seventh Chakra

Sahasrara

the seventh chakra assessment

Assess the vitality of this aspect of your life energy system. Place an "X" under the number that best represents the current status of each statement for you. Five is the highest ranking of level of truth. One represents the lowest level.

	1	2	3	4	5
I do not over-intellectualize.					
I understand the difference between spirituality and religion. I take responsibility for my spiritual growth.					
I easily perceive, analyze and assimilate information.					
I do not suffer from confusion. There is clarity in my life.					
I understand the role of my beliefs in my life.					
I learn easily.					
I know my behaviors and thoughts extend out into all living things in the universe and I take responsibility for this.					
I move gracefully in my body and through life's experiences.					
I apply attention to my inner thoughts and fantasies and seek a deeper understanding of myself through the exploration of them.					
People and relationships are more important to me than things.					
My peace and joy come from within.					
I am fully aware of the purpose of my life and how I can best serve others.					
I understand group consciousness and my role in it.					
I trust the wisdom of the universe and I remain unattached to controlling outcomes.					
I choose happiness over the need to be right.					
I can be a 'witness' to the events of my life, expressing both objective and subjective observations.					
I take responsibility for what I have in my life.					
I see that the situations in my life are a reflection of my own energy.					
I know and am living the legacy that I wish to leave the world.					
I enjoy silence.					

Total of all Columns

Guide for Results:

80 – 100:   Your vital energy in this chakra center is excellent at this time. Review the chapter to maintain your healthy balance.

60 – 79:   Your vital energy in this chakra center is good at this time. Take some actions to increase your possibilities and energy levels.

40 – 59:   Are you experiencing difficulties in certain areas of your life? Focus on this chakra to begin to balance and re-energize yourself.

20 – 39:   Your vital energy is zapped in this chakra. Take some action today!

0 – 19:   Yikes! Get into action now. You may want to seek professional counsel.

seventh chakra assessment questions

1. Which statements caught you off-guard, made you slightly uncomfortable, raised an eyebrow or caught your attention?

2. How do you feel after doing this assessment?

3. What areas of the assessment do you feel confident about?

4. What aspects of the assessment raised an emotional reaction in you? If so, what was your response?

5. What areas do you see that you might want to put some attention on releasing, healing, fixing, or creating? Please list these with three steps to support your growth in each area.

the seventh chakra: sahasrara

*T*he seventh chakra, named Sahasrara, is located at the crown of the head. It is the gateway to the universal energy and a spiritual life. The color of this chakra is sometimes referred to as violet, white or all the lower colors incorporated as an integrated multicolored symbol. The element of this chakra is thought. Thought is used as a vehicle for increasing the levels of self-awareness and consciousness. In the seventh chakra, all the aspects of the spiritual being are integrated. By increasing one's awareness of the power of the mind, one becomes more conscious of who they are and how they create an open channel to connect with spiritual energy. The seventh chakra is about being open, expansive, present, and embracing the web of the universe. It is here that one opens to the experience and deep understanding to the meaning of spiritual bliss.

The pace of Western life is busier than ever. People are in motion, doing and thinking, most of the time. The mind is constantly active filling almost every moment of the day with thoughts. The average person may experience up to 15,000 thoughts per day. Some of these thoughts may be filled with promise, positive affirmations, possibility, love and joy. For many people, the majority of their thoughts are about worries, regrets about the past, concerns about the future, or fear-based thoughts generated from the ego. Thoughts play a major role in how one creates and lives life. What we think plays a role in what we believe, perceive and imagine as reality.

"Life is what happens while you are making other plans."

John Lennon

The world is turning into a society based on computers and information exchanges. The World Wide Web now connects people across the globe. The exchange of information that once took a great length of time now can be transferred with a push of a button on a keyboard. The transfer of information and exchange of communication is happening faster than ever. Obtaining and storing information equates power and wealth.

Cell phones, Palm Pilots, laptops and other high tech equipment are standard items in the home of many people in Western society. People are consumed with gadgets and toys that will provide speedy solutions and convenience, claiming to streamline one's life. These gadgets have become key instruments in many peoples already packed lives. For many, their day is filled with the sorting and assimilating of information, digesting knowledge and taking care of the many details of day-to-day life. Life is fast paced and filled with convenient tools to simplify.

Yet, life has not become simple for many. The human mind is constantly thinking about the various agendas of the day and life in general. Throughout a day the mind may be filled with projections about what might happen, what could have happened and what needs to happen, both in the personal and professional arena. On top of these processes, the basic needs of life take up many thoughts as the mind determines when to eat, what to eat, how to eat, and who to eat with. Assessments and decisions are constantly being made. Judgments and predictions of other people's characteristics are constantly being mulled over. In essence, the mind is a human computer that never rests.

An active mind is a healthy mind. The intellect is stretched and strengthened when it experiences challenges. To learn easily and well is a sign of a balanced seventh chakra. Yet over-use of the mind is common. The human mind is not a computer. It is much more powerful. A computer can only share the knowledge that it can find within the system that it is connected to. A computer cannot tap into or create new ways to think and interpret. A mind that is too active may function in the same way. If the mind becomes conditioned to depend on the ego and rational thought, the mind loses its capacity to tap into another source of wisdom and knowledge that is much greater. A mind that is too busy thinking fails to truly step into experiencing life fully. Instead, a life of distance, calculations and processing occurs. The rhythm of life itself is replaced by the need to know through hard facts and information.

In such a busy information-based world slowing down life can be a challenge. Moving from actively and constantly thinking to non-thinking can be a big leap. Yet, as with any practice, it is doable. For many, the first step is increasing one's awareness of the activity of the mind. Self-awareness is to deepen one's understanding and observation of one's self. In doing this one can see clearly who they are and how they live from the perspective of being an objective observer. To observe the self without judgment or justifications, but as a human experience, allows one to step into a position of greater choice. In the sixth chakra you practiced the art of seeing life patterns and perspectives. As you continue to observe yourself you become more aware of the quantity and quality of your thoughts. By observing your thoughts you can understand the beliefs that are developed and how these beliefs create life experiences.

A belief system is a set of thoughts (or beliefs) that support the perception of what one may hold to be true in the world. By shifting the core "limiting" beliefs and thoughts of what one thinks to be true, one can shift their experience of life. As long as there is a belief that things happen a certain way or

"We do not learn by experience, but by our capacity for experience."
Buddha

that things will always be a certain way, an attachment to an outcome is present. There is a preconceived notion of how things will be based on past experiences. These attachments remove one from the flow of life and from experiencing life free of the need of the ego to control and manipulate through "knowing" outcomes, so that the ego can feel free and safe.

As limiting beliefs and attachments that do not support you in living your life are released, you begin to empty the mind, release the power of the ego, and open to the universal connection. You release attachments so that you can experience the world in a truly open manner. This experience, of living free of attachments and limiting beliefs, allows one to live in the moment and to connect with a knowledge that all turns out in the world as it needs to. One realizes that there is no need to control anything. Instead one learns to set intentions with positive affirmations on that which they seek to experience. Then, the flow of live is experienced, moment to moment, and the magic of what life presents is embraced.

In the early 1900's most people did not believe that a human could go to the moon. More than likely, few even entertained the idea. It took the dedication of many people believing that traveling to the moon was possible for it to become a reality. Now, in today's world, no one lives with the limiting belief that this act is impossible. Many trips have successfully been made to the moon. If the scientists had not stretched the concept of what was believed to be possible, this may have never occurred.

Sir Edmund Hillary believed that he could climb Mount Everest; the rest of the world thought his vision to be impossible. After three attempts he made it to the top of Everest. The perceived limits of reality for many people shifted because someone else believed that reaching the top of Mount Everest was possible. Today thousands of people have followed Sir Edmund Hillary's footsteps. Olympic athletes also provide great examples of the power of thought and belief. Year after year athletes become quicker, more agile and stronger. Each year they break existing world records. Because these athletes are focused on possibilities, they set the stage for the event to occur, for records to be broken and for what once was thought impossible to be possible. The belief that any limitations existed to reaching their goal was not part of their consciousness.

Explore your thoughts and how they support you in creating what you want in life. If your thoughts are based on what is not possible most likely it will not be possible for you to achieve your vision easily. If on the other hand you feel that you can create anything and that the universe is playing a role in your life path, you will flow in the direction of your dreams. The core beliefs you hold about yourself are the thoughts that create your world. In releasing the mind of the constraints of limiting beliefs and ego driven thoughts one can more easily step into moving through life open to the direction and guidance of spirit and the universe. One becomes less attached to having to know how life is going to unfold. Instead one is able to step into life and live each moment of the day.

To life a live based on thoughts that are positive and affirming creates a life of the same energy. To live a life based on thoughts of the magic and wonders that can mysteriously emerge in one's life creates a life that playfully anticipates these events. Thoughts of compassion and love beget compassion and love. These thoughts create a life path that one skips along versus a path of push and pull, struggle and suffering. Our thoughts create our world.

In the lower chakras you focused on the body as a source of information for your earthly experience. You developed your ability to feel sensations within your body. This helped you to connect to your body wisdom. You also observed and developed the skill to sense the energy of your environment and of others. This helped you with your intuition. And, finally, you melded the body and mind together as you explored your intention and how you create your experiences from your intentions. Now, in the seventh chakra your beliefs are the foundation of the whole experience you create in the world. Through this process you deepened your understanding of who you are and how you create or limit yourself in life.

The seventh chakra energy is also about the experience of being a spiritual being. You may explore the mind to understand your thought processes. Then to become free of the demands of the ego mind, you let go of the thought process and analyzing. It is here that you let go of the notion that you are your body, your mind, your thoughts, your ego, or your emotions. You are indeed something much greater that all that. You are everything and you are nothing, all at the same time. You are what you experience in the very moment. You are a moving mass of expression connected to all that is in the world and universe. You are what you experience in a moment — then it changes. When you live your life from this state and point of view, you have shifted from an overly active state of mind to a present state of mind. You have entered into the experience of "being." To experience the state of being, the desire to understand decreases. Instead the experience of the moment and the observation of self in the moment becomes more predominate. In this state, you experience spirit, directly, in each moment.

The seventh chakra focuses on shifting the mind and opening the crown of the head to the energies of the greater power, God, spirit or the universe. To

" — impulses of energy and information that we experience as thoughts' are the raw material of the universe."
Deepak Chopra, MD

" — to live life fully, we must learn to let go of all our chronic thought flows, all our convoluted religious concepts, all our superstitious fantasies and theological beliefs systems-and encounter the depths and heights of spiritual life directly, through our immediate experience."
John Selby,
Kundalini Awakening

open to this power is to step into fully experiencing life in partnership with the invisible web of energy that holds us all together. As one trusts this force that is intangible, one develops a deep sense of knowing that is not solely based on information or knowledge, it is based on an inner experience and deep connection and trust to the flow of life. Wisdom is experienced when one consciously steps into this deep sense of knowing that is absent of information and processes geared around having to think. Opening the seventh chakra allows the wisdom of all the ages to come through the body and into the physical world. From that place one can easily learn and process information while remaining unattached to having to know or control any situation in life.

Thoughts are powerful elements that set the course of one's life. There are thoughts that we are aware of and there are thoughts that we are unaware of. Yet, many times the most powerful source of wisdom comes from letting go of thought. It is in silence that one often finds the answers to the situations that they seek. The body and mind work together to achieve silence. As you increase you ability to sense the subtle energy shifts of the body you also deepen your understanding of what thoughts you hold that create these sensations. To train the body and the mind to find silence is the gateway to opening the seventh chakra. For many this process includes a form of meditation, a quieting of the mind. In meditation, thoughts are released so that peace and space enters into the body and soul. Exploring the space between thoughts opens the mind to other realms of possibilities. The space allows one to tap into the wisdom of the universe. There is a saying: "There is no new information in the universe." If so, then shouldn't anyone be able to tap into any information that is in the layer of universal energy at any time? The act of being without thought allows for one's consciousness to expand and grow and to be open to connecting with this greater power and source.

The process of becoming quiet leads one to discover and reconnect to the soul. Becoming quiet is not an easy task. Taming the mind and releasing the ego can take years for some people to achieve. Yet, as one explores and practices the art of becoming quiet through meditation, one learns to release the core thoughts and beliefs that create suffering and unhappiness. These thoughts are released and the ego is excused. Peace, compassion and tranquility follow. One realizes the unlimited and the limitlessness of being and the simplicity of life. In this realization a new level of responsibility and respect for life itself emerges. The once assertive ego-based thoughts are replaced with kind and loving thoughts. One more easily accepts what "is" in life instead of seeking and searching for something else.. One becomes still to the experience of life through the body, mind and spirit.

" — those who achieve inner silence are also thinking in the ordinary way. But the thought takes place against a background of non-thought."

Deepak Chopra,
How to Know God

"I regard soul as the sense of feeling in a person of being part of a larger or universal order. Such a feeling must arise from the actual experience of being part of or connected in some vital or spiritual way to the universe."
Alexander Lowen, M.D.,
Bioenergetics

In the seventh chakra you embrace the oneness and infinity of the world and your existence. It is here that you integrate the spirit with your life's work. It is in the seventh chakra that one releases any attachment of the mind so that one's uniqueness and purpose can shine through to serve the greater good. The energy of the seventh chakra is about fully accepting and embracing what spirit has put us here to experience and share with others. You are humble, accepting and choose to live without suffering. You develop the ability to be fully present to what is. You choose to have more space in your outer world and your inner world — your mind, emotions and thoughts. You learn the power of becoming unattached to knowledge and thoughts and material possessions. You embrace the ability to become the silent observer of yourself without judgment. You develop a deep sense of self and soul.

It is here, in the seventh chakra, that you decide to rise above all the chaos of ego-driven desires to embrace the unity of your existence and the endlessness of your existence. It is here that you step aside and allow the universe to work through you, to serve and to be fully aware and engaged as your spirit is connected with the energy of the universe. It is here that you experience a peaceful inner existence.

"We are not human beings having a spiritual experience, but rather spiritual beings having a human experience."

Pierre Tielhard de Chardin

seventh chakra details

Element:	Thought
Sanskrit:	Sahasrara, immortal self, Thousand fold lotus flower
Color:	Rainbow of all chakra colors
Location:	Top of head at the crown
Corresponding areas:	Upper brain, central nervous system, pituitary gland
Theme:	Consciousness and beliefs
Core Shift:	I tap in to the universal energy of knowing, learning and being
Challenge:	Explore and release personal beliefs that are limiting

Balanced Characteristics:
Individual has a strong sense of spirituality and lives an existence exclusive of ego.

Signs of Imbalance:

Too much/Expanded	*Too little/Contracted*
Overly intellectual	Learning difficulties
Confusion	Rigid belief system
Dissociation from the body	Apathy
Constantly thinking/processing knowledge	Materialistic
Obsessive thinking	Lacks desire for spiritual-exploration and self-knowledge
Over-use of spiritual concepts	

Physical Symptoms:

Chronic exhaustion	Brain tumors
Alzheimer's Disease	Cognitive delusions
Epilepsy	

Signs of Balance:
- Perceived as having a high level of awareness
- Lives life engaged with spirituality
- Has a high level of consciousness
- Demonstrates a high level of wisdom
- Feels connected to all life and the universal energy
- Is unattached to outcomes, how people are and how life unfolds
- Seeks silence as a source of knowledge and wisdom
- Has explored beliefs and how one creates through beliefs
- Learns easily and enjoys engaging the mind

Goal:

ల To expand your consciousness, to live free of limiting beliefs and to be fully engaged with your life purpose

Activities to explore:

ల Develop spiritual disciplines

ల Develop a meditation practice

ల Explore belief systems

ల Use programs that promote a means of learning and studying

ల Learn the process of connecting with the language and intelligence of the body

ల Learn the art of doing nothing

ల Learn the art of being without thought

ల Explore your vision, mission and purpose in life

ల Live a life oriented around purpose and service

shifts for the seventh chakra

From...	To...
"I have difficulties making decisions."	"I can question things and come to conclusions for myself."
"It is my way or the highway."	"I am open-minded and able to ask questions and evaluate easily."
"It's all about me and my plans and my things."	"It really is about a deeper connection and interactions with others, the environment, and spirit."
"My concerns are focused on my world."	"Every action I take plays a part in the greater whole."
"My thoughts, actions and words are not relevant in the scheme of things."	"I belong to a web that connects what I say, do and think."
"My focus is on what happens around me and how it affects me."	"I am thoughtful and aware of the happenings of others."
"I look for results to validate who I am."	"Where I am is where I am."
"My mind won't shut up."	"I find peace in emptiness."
"I must consume knowledge."	"I have everything I need to know."
"There is so much I need to do."	"There is only the moment."
"I have difficulty learning new things."	"I learn easily and gracefully."
"I have no reason for living."	"I am fully engaged in a purposeful and rewarding life."
"I have little awareness of my inner self."	"I practice self awareness daily."
"I must know_____."	"I practice 'being' versus knowing."
Life is hard and full of struggle. I feel alone.	"Spirit guides me through life."

Questions for journal work:

- How do you define your spirituality?
- What is your philosophy about meditation?
- What are your challenges with meditation?
- How do you seek knowledge and why?
- How do you define wisdom?
- What are you most attached to in life? What must you have?
- How would your life be different if you let go of these attachments?
- What have you not achieved in your life that you would like to achieve? What are the limiting beliefs you hold about accomplishing your vision?
- Where do thoughts come from?
- What do you find when you enter into the space between thoughts?
- How do you let wisdom and universal knowledge come through you?
- What brings you the greatest level of peace?

∽ How are you of service to others?

∽ What are you willing to let go of along your path of spiritual growth?

Keywords:

Consciousness	Belief systems	Intelligence
Unity	Transcendence	Awareness
Universal connection	Cosmic energy	Thought
Space		

engaging the seventh chakra energy

The seventh chakra is the chakra that integrates the energies of all of the other chakras. It is here that one learns to be more mindful and aware and to live a more spiritually based life. To accomplish this, one must learn how to quiet the mind through acknowledging sensations of the body and the undercurrent of thoughts that support these sensations. As we become more present to our own self and the sensations and energies we are expressing we become more present in every moment of life.

You have explored many exercises that have helped you to begin to be more in touch with your energy body. The meditation below is designed for a full session of awareness and activation for all of the chakras. This meditation includes the use of mantras, the breath and visualization and intention to release and observe the energy flow within and between each chakra center. Proceed through each chakra using as many or as few breaths as necessary to facilitate the energy movement that feels appropriate for you. Let your intuition guide you. The key is to be present and grounded through the process, yet open to the energy of your system and the universe simultaneously. It is key to observe your sensations, use your breath and be fully present to the process. Listen to your body and do as much or as little as feels best for you. As you become more familiar with the process, you may want to lengthen your meditation time.

Use the Daily Root Meditation, on page 34, to become centered and grounded in your body.

Once you feel grounded, bring your awareness to your first chakra. Bring a nice deep breath inward. As you release the breath emit the sound of LAM (lahm) and let the vibration of this seed word move through your whole being, traveling out your throat. At the same time as you are exhaling, tighten your gluteal and sphincter muscles. Imagine yourself wringing out and releasing any energy blocks in this area of your body. Pause at the bottom of your breath and release your contracted muscles. Then, as you inhale, bring all your awareness to the first chakra area, observing the energy as it moves and flows in your body. Imagine the red, four-petal shaped chakra sitting deeply within your pelvic floor as you inhale. Observe the energy flows. Repeat this process of exhaling and tightening, then inhaling and relaxing your muscles while visualizing the symbols and colors, as many times as feels appropriate and comfortable.

During your last inhale breath of the first chakra shift your attention to the second chakra, drawing energy up from the first to the second chakra. Bring your awareness to your second chakra area, your sexual organs and genitals.

As you begin to exhale, stimulate your second chakra with the use of the seed word VAM (vahm). As you exhale, tighten and contract the muscles related to your sexual organs. Pause at the end of your exhale and release your contracted muscles. As you begin to inhale, observe the energy entering into your body. Embrace this wonderful flow of energy as you visualize the orange six-petal symbol for the second chakra. Repeat the breath and contractions of your muscles, as you like, pausing at the end of the exhaled breath and inhaled breath to observe the sensations and movement of energy in your body.

Repeat this same process of observing the body and using the breath to engage the third chakra, using the seed word RAM (rahm). Constrict all the muscles related to the first, second and third chakras, the sphincter, gluteal, sexual organs, and the stomach muscles as you exhale. Pause at the end of your exhale, release your contracted muscle and observe the energy sensations within your body. Let the energy flow and move from both below and above you through all of your chakra centers. As you inhale, imagine the color yellow and the third chakra symbol sitting in your third chakra area. Repeat your breath, the contractions and visualizations as many times as you like.

Repeat the same breathing process for the fourth chakra center. Bring your arms out to your sides, arms parallel to the floor and palms up as you exhale and release the seed word of YAM (yahm). Once you begin your inhale, imagine your energy body fully open and connected to all the loving energy that is available to you. Open your heart to the world and imagine the fourth chakra symbol and color green in the heart chakra as you feel the expansion. Again, remember to pause at the bottom of your exhale and at the top of the inhale. Simply observe as you breathe slowly, for as many times as you like.

As you inhale your next breath, pull the energy up to your throat chakra. Bring all your awareness to your throat and the vibration you feel as you release the seed word HAM (hahm). As you shift to your inhale, imagine the fifth chakra symbol with the color blue on your throat chakra as you focus on the energy movement and your breath. Imagine and focus on the energy of your body moving upward through all of the chakras. Repeat this process as many times as you intuit your body and energy would like.

As you proceed to the sixth chakra use the seed word OM (ohm). As you exhale imagine the higher energies moving through your sixth chakra to the vibration of OM. Pause at the bottom of your exhale. Then as you inhale, bring the symbol and indigo blue color of the sixth chakra to your mind's eye and observe as energy moves through your whole system. Notice how all of the centers have become more open, flowing and activated.

As you bring your awareness to the crown chakra, feel the energy flowing throughout your whole energy body, sensing and observing continuously. Imagine the universal energy coming into your body - meeting the rising flow of the kundalini energy opened up and moving from the first through the sixth chakras. Hold a harmonious space as these energies merge and deeply connect you to your own energy body and the universal energy simultaneously. Breathe deeply as you enjoy the flow of energy and vitality in your body and spirit. Immerse yourself in the powerful sensations of being fully present and flowing energetically.

Slowly open your eyes and bring your awareness back into the room as you continue to feel this powerful flow and connection within yourself. Wiggle your toes and roll your ankles to remind yourself to be fully grounded and connected to the earth energy. Shake your hands and arms and bend over as you shake off any excess energy. Maintain your awareness of your center and core energy flow as you move throughout the day.

my seventh chakra summary

1. The insights I have about my seventh chakra are...

2. What I would like to focus on with regard to the seventh chakra is...

3. The three things I am willing to do to bring this chakra into balance and vitality are...

    1.

    2.

    3.

4. The behaviors and patterns I am willing to process, explore, release or give up are...

5. I am grateful for...

bibliography

Body/Energy/Chakra

Anand, Margo. *The Art of Sexual Ecstasy*. Jermemy P. Tarcher, 1989.

Brennan, Barbara Ann. *Hands of Light*. Bantam Books, 1988.

Chitty, John and Muller, Mary Louise. *Energy Exercise*s. Polarity Press, 1990.

Dewhurst-Maddock, Olivea. *Healing with Sound*. Gaia Books Unlimited, 1997.

Eden, Donna. *Energy Medicine*. Jeremy P. Tarrcher/Putman, 1998.

Gendlin Ph. D., Eugene. *Focusing*. Bantam Books, 1981.

Jarow, Rick. *Creating the Work You Love*. Destiny Books, 1995.

Judith, Anodea. *Wheels of Life*. Llewellyn New Times, 1989.

Judith, Anodea. *Eastern Body Western Mind*. Celestial Arts Publishing, 1996.

Judith, Anodea, and Susan Vegas. *The Sevenfold Journey*. The Crossing Press, 1997.

Leadbeater C.W. *The Chakras*. The Theosophical Publishing House, 1927.

Lowen M.D., Alexander. *Bioenergetics*. Penguin Books, 1976.

Myss, Caroline. *Anatomy of the Spirit*. XXXX

Naparstek, Belleruth. *Your Sixth Sense*, Harper Collins, 1997,

Orloff, M.D., Judith. *Intuitive Healing*. Three Rivers Press, 2000.

Oshman, Jim L. *Energy Medicine*. The Scientific Basis. Churchill Livingstone, 2000.

Putnoi, Johanna. *Senses Wide Open*, Ulysses Press, 2000.

Sarada, Jaya. *The Path of Return*. Grace Publishing, 2001.

Selby, John. *Kundilini Awakening*. Bantam Press, 1992.

Sills, Franklyn. *The Polarity Process*. Element, 1989.

Simpson, Liz. *The Book of Chakra Healin*g. Gaia Books Unlimited, 1997.

Strozzi Heckler, Richard. *The Anatomy of Change*. North American Press, 1993.

Weiser Cornell, Ph.D., Ann. *The Power of Focusing*. MJF Books, 1996.

Personal Development:

Beck, Martha, *Finding Your Own North Star*. Random House, 2001.

Britten, Rhonda, *Fearless Living*. Dutton, 2001.

Capacchione, PhD., Lucia. *Visioning*. Jeremy P. Tarcher/Putman, 2000.

Cameron, Julia, *The Artist's Way*. Jeremy P. Tarcher/Putman, 1992.

Dalai Lama and Howard C. Culter, M.D. *The Art of Happiness*. Riverhead Books, 1998.

Ford, Debbie. *Dark Side of the Light Chasers*. Riverhead Books, 1999.

Ruiz Don Miguel. *The Four Agreements*. Amber-Allen Publishing, 1997.

Tolle, Eckhardt. *The Power of Now*. New World Library, 1999.

Williamson, Marianne. *A Return to Love*. Harper Collins, 1992.

Zukav, Gary. *The Seat of the Soul*. Simon and Schuster, 1989.

Pathways to Radiance

Kathy Pike of Pathways to Radiance, LLC inspires individuals to expand their awareness of energy and body wisdom for personal and professional growth through coaching, teleclasses, and workshops.

Pathways to Radiance works with individuals in helping professions, corporations, schools and other organizations. For more information on the services and products provided by Pathways to Radiance, please visit the following websites:

www.PathwaystoRadiance.com
www.coachpike.com